ALL
DU
MONEY

INSURANCE: ARE YOU COVERED?

ALLIED DUNBAR

MONEY GUIDES

INSURANCE: ARE YOU COVERED?

MIHIR BOSE

Longman

© Allied Dunbar Financial Services Limited 1988

ISBN 0–85121–417–7

Published by

Longman Professional and Business Communications Division
Longman Group UK Limited
21–27 Lamb's Conduit Street, London WC1N 3NJ

Associated Offices

Australia Longman Professional Publishing (Pty) Limited
130 Philip Street, Sydney, NSW 2000

Hong Kong Longman Group (Far East) Limited
Cronwall House, 18th Floor, Taikoo Trading Estate,
Tong Chong Street, Quarry Bay

Malaysia Longman Malaysia Sdn Bhd
No 3 Jalan Kilan A, Off Jalan Penchala,
Petaling Jaya, Selangor, Malaysia

Singapore Longman Singapore Publshers (Pte) Ltd
25 First Lok Yang Road, Singapore 2262

USA Longman Group (USA) Inc
500 North Dearborn Street, Chicago, Illinois 60610

All rights reserved. No part of this publication may be reproduced, stored in a retrieval system, or transmitted, in any form or by any means, electronic, mechanical, photocopying, recording or otherwise, without either the prior written permission of the copyright holder for which application should be addressed in the first instance to the publishers or a licence permitting restricted copying issued by the Copyright Licensing Agency Ltd, 33–34 Alfred Place, London WC1E 7DP.

No responsibility for loss occasioned to any person acting or refraining from action as a result of the material in this publication can be accepted by the author or publishers.

The views and opinions of Allied Dunbar may not necessarily coincide with some of the views and opinions expressed in this book which are solely those of the authors and no endorsement of them by Allied Dunbar should be inferred.

A CIP catalogue record for this book is available from the British Library.

Printed in Great Britain by Biddles Ltd, Guildford, Surrey.

Mihir Bose

Mihir Bose is a freelance writer and broadcaster. After obtaining a degree in Maths and Physics and qualifying as a chartered accountant, he finally summoned courage in 1974 to follow the profession he always wanted – journalism. He was the first cricket correspondent of *London Broadcasting* and then moved on to write for *The Sunday Times* firstly for the foreign desk and later on for sport and general news. He continues to write about cricket and soccer for *The Sunday Times* but devotes most of his time these days to write on financial topics. He has written for all the major national newspapers and edited various publications including *Property Guide and Pensions*. He was deputy editor of *Financial Weekly* and City Features Editor of *London Daily News*. Since its closure he has been a full-time freelance writer dividing his time between contributing regularly to *The Guardian* and *The Financial Times* and broadcast work with the BBC and LBC.

He has also written six other books: three on his favourite subject of cricket, a biography of Subhas Bose the Indian nationalist, a history of the Aga Khan family and a study of the October crash. He makes up for his failure to have captained Surrey by captaining a journalists' cricket team of such widely varying talents that they can never be insured against defeat!

Dedication

To Kalpana

Introduction

Insurance is a subject that conjures up contrasting pictures. Either we have the vision of an Edward Robinson-type character trying to probe how a husband did away with his wife in order to claim on life insurance – a subject that has provided Hollywood with some startlingly effective movies – or we think about pushy salesmen trying to sell us policies we do not need or understand. On screen the theme of insurance fraud can provide gripping drama; off screen it seems to be a nuisance that produces a yawn or much cynical comment.

Both reactions are understandable, but neither is justified. In the modern world we need insurance and know frighteningly little about it. I must confess that in the course of researching and writing this book I discovered insurance facts that I did not know existed. I also became aware of the many areas of life for which we are not adequately covered and where an insurance policy could help provide both the vital peace of mind and the protection we clearly need. This book is a guide to everyday insurance needs – what you ought to have and how you can go about getting it.

I am indebted to many friends and colleagues for their help and assistance in the course of writing this book. Hugh Pym, who can occasionally be a frustrating bowler to captain in our class of cricket – like us all he would benefit from a higher standard of play – has been a marvellous friend and without his infectious enthusiasm I would not have had the opportunity to write this book. His wonderful wife Susan, whose tuck shop is a legendary institution in our cricket world – and for which, I suspect, she does not carry adequate insurance – was, in her very different way, just as helpful.

Many people in the industry freely gave their time to help me understand this often complicated subject and I must thank, in particular, Ron Spill of the Legal & General, Mark Daniels of Equitable Life and Chris Woodhams of Greig Middleton Financial Services. Hyman Wolanski and his long-suffering partner Michael Posner showed great patience as they answered my many queries. What Hyman does not know about pensions is not worth knowing, but you would expect that from a man who has the good sense to be a Tottenham Hotspur supporter. David Parish of Carlton Financial Planning Ltd, despite being a Chelsea supporter, was extremely generous with his time and wonderfully helpful in explaining the problems faced by the independent financial adviser. I must also, of course, thank the men from Allied Dunbar, David Vessey and Clifford Green who showed a patience above and beyond the call of duty.

Above all, this book would hardly have been possible, or would at least have taken twice as much effort, but for my faithful Amstrad – a marvellous gift from my sister Panna and brother-in-law Tapan, who is truly a man of insurance.

Contents

1 The background to insurance

Insurance is a form of protection. In very simple terms it involves a large number of people paying money into a common fund. How much they pay depends on what they are trying to protect and their individual circumstances. This common fund is invested and when one of the investors suffers a loss, he or she receives a certain sum to compensate them for the damage. Insurance cannot protect us from the bad things in life, but it can provide us money to alleviate the pain and to possibly recreate what we have lost.

The earliest form of insurance known to man was probably marine insurance. The ancient Greeks and the ancient Phoenicians – both great sailors – certainly insured their ships and cargoes. So well established was the idea that in 533 AD the Byzantine Emperor Justinian exempted 'nautical usury' from the general law that interest rates could not go up above 6% . One wishes there was such a Byzantine law about interest rates now.

Bottoms up

In those days marine insurance took the form of what is known as bottomry. This was a loan against a ship's bottom – if the ship was lost, the loan was lost. If the ship returned then the loan was repaid along with a reward. Marine insurance received a tremendous boost in the 16th century as the European powers expanded their trade and their empires acquired colonies worldwide. Ships sailed all over the world exploring and exploiting continents, discovering riches and occasionally ending their voyages at the bottom of the sea or shipwrecked off some inhospitable coast. The rise of Italy's sea power provided a boost to marine insurance and as the banking and other business skills of the Italians transferred to London – Lombard Street owes its name to the Lombardy region of Italy – so did the principle of insuring ships. Ship owners paid a premium to underwriters and if a cargo was lost a claim was made.

Fire insurance

In 1666 the reach of insurance widened with the Great Fire of London. This not only changed London it made people aware of how quickly and devastatingly they could lose their homes, their possessions – everything they valued. In 1680 the first insurance company providing fire cover, called The Fire Office or Phoenix (not related to the company of the same name today) was established. In 1710 came the Sun Fire Office which still exists. The principle of marine insurance was applied: people paid premiums to build up a large fund from which payments were made to those who had fires. The security or protection this gave them was known as cover.

Life insurance

Life insurance also owes its origins to Italy, though in this case the Romans were responsible. History records that one of the earliest mutual clubs was 'The Hornblowers', formed in 203 AD in Algeria by a Roman garrison. The club was opened to all Roman legionary officers who paid monthly contributions into a central fund. On death, promotion, transfer or becoming a veteran they were granted 500 denarii, the Roman currency, but this was reduced by half if they were dismissed or demoted. The Romans also developed the annuity where in return for a single payment, a person received regular income.

Medieval times saw the formation of guilds to provide some protection for those who left the land to seek work or to set up in business. In exchange for contribution members were entitled to a loan or a subsidy whenever things went wrong. If a member fell ill, or had no customers, if his wife was unwell, or his daughter came of age, or he became widowed, the guild gave him money. It was never a great deal but it lasted for a lifetime.

The 16th century development of marine and fire insurance also contained a form of life insurance. The premium was a flat rate for a wide range of ages and the contracts were always for one year. A company called the Amicable Society also provided a small death benefit. Granted a charter in 1706 its purpose was to secure 2,000 subscribers paying £6.4s each. This was on the understanding that £10,000, £5 per subscriber, would be shared between the nominees of those subscribers who had died during the year. The Amicable later became part of the Norwich which exists to this day.

The story goes that the Amicable would only extend insurance to those under the age of 45. A schoolmaster and mathematician called James Dodson who was above this age was denied cover and decided to remedy this. An expert in mathematics, he had written books on it and was a member of the Royal Society. He used the theory of probability to work out the basis of what has come to be known as life assurance.

The principle that Dodson used was quite simple. If a group of people all aged 30 decided to take out life assurance paying the same sum, then it was reasonable to assume that few of them would die in the early years. At that age premiums paid would exceed claims made. However, as the years went by and the people got older there would come a time when claims would exceed premium. So the early premiums must be stored and invested to earn interest. The interest earned would be allocated to the individuals by means of a bonus declaration. Dodson himself assumed a 3% rate of interest per annum and reduced the premiums accordingly.

Although life assurance has varied greatly throughout the years,(as we shall see) the basic principle laid down by Dodson is still valid. It remains a case of premiums being collected to provide funds that back the long term contracts, and it is from these funds that benefits are paid. Dodson's critics alleged that his plan would never work – the life assurance premiums calculated by Dodson were so low compared to rates prevailing then that it was widely believed that any scheme based on such figures would fail. In fact, Dodson had used the mean number of burials for the years 1728–50. These were years of severe weather and high deaths due to famines, and the widespread use of cheap gin which wreaked havoc with peoples' lives. If anything Dodson's premiums, compared to our times, seemed very high. The petition for a Royal charter made it clear that 'extra premiums were to be charged for hazardous occupations and/or females aged between eight and 50'.

The petition raised a storm of protest with much opposition from existing companies including the Amicable. Dodson died soon after the charter was presented and after much debate it was denied. The petitioners then decided to form a mutual society and the Society for Equitable Assurances on Lives and Survivorships was set up in 1762. It has since become The Equitable Life Assurance Society and was the first life assurance society to grant long term contracts of life assurance for either a stated period or the whole of life with premiums calculated according to age and type of assurance.

It is important to mention the difference between *insurance* and *assurance*. You can insure against the possibility of something happening, but it must be possible for the event *not* to happen. Assurance concerns making provisions for when an event does occur. Hence the term life assurance –

we will all die sometime. However, to keep matters simple, the term insurance is used throughout this book.

What sort of company?

Equitable, by its very structure, is a mutual company where the profits go back to the policyholders as there are no shareholders. The other form of insurance company is the proprietary type with shareholders who have a stake in the company and are entitled to share in its profits. This is also the structure for most types of commercial firms. Proprietary life insurance companies are often public companies quoted on the London stock exchange. Equitable is one of a small number of companies who do not pay commission to other people to sell their products. Most other life companies pay commissions and the methods by which such commissions are paid cause great controversy, as we shall see. Insurance is also available from a composite insurance company (this sells life, pensions and general insurance like motor insurance and household contents), or from friendly societies and provident associations with subscribing members and other non-profit making bodies. Insurance cover is also available through Lloyd's brokers, a specialised form of broker which will be discussed later (see Chapter 15).

As far as you are concerned it should make no difference whether the company with which you take out insurance is a mutual or a proprietary company, sells only life insurance or all kinds of insurance. You will often read claims by one sort of insurance company that it is better than another. There is some research claiming that over the years mutual life assurance companies have shown a better investment track record but there is nothing conclusive about this.

What you need to make sure is that the insurance company you are dealing with is authorised by the **Department of**

Trade and Industry (DTI). This you can do by contacting the DTI's Insurance Division, 10–18 Victoria Street, London SW1H ONN (Tel: (01) 215 3106). There are about 840 companies authorized in this country. Companies are required to send in returns each year and the DTI check whether they are maintaining the solvency requirements which are necessary for the company to carry on business. Each year one or two companies fail to meet the test.

Brokers

It is very likely that when you take out an insurance policy you will go through a middleman known as a broker rather than deal directly with the company. There was a time when the word 'broker' had a very unfortunate connotation. At the time of the South Sea bubble in the early part of the 18th century, being a broker was almost synonymous with being a crook, a shark or a rogue. Men who performed all the functions associated with brokers did not like being called by that name and preferred being called 'office keepers'.

Many things have changed since then and with the Financial Services Act now in force brokers are suddenly part of a new, tougher world. Before the Financial Services Act (in April 1988) there were three types of intermediary or middlemen: starting with independent advisers who could, in theory, offer you all the products available on the market, the part-time agent (often a solicitor or chartered accountant) and the tied representative. Distinguishing between the three brought problems as their roles overlapped and it was difficult for the customer to appreciate the differences. This continues to be the case with general insurance, but with life insurance the situation is becoming clearer.

Under the Financial Services Act the life insurance broker can be a full-time independent broker registered either with **Financial Intermediaries, Managers and Brokers**

Regulatory Association (FIMBRA) or directly with the **Securities and Investment Board (SIB)**, the watchdog organisation set up by the Financial Services Act.

The part-time agents such as solicitors and accountants are authorised by their professional bodies, such as the Law Society or the Chartered Accountancy Institute, depending on how much of their business comes from selling insurance and offering investment.

Tied agents are employed by a particular insurance company and are called company representatives. They are authorised to sell only the company's products. However, it is possible that if you ask a company representative to obtain a policy from a company other than the one he represents, under the law he may be allowed to introduce you to someone who can arrange this for you, but it is a tricky area.

If you want to check whether a broker is authorised then you can check by contacting FIMBRA at Hertsmere House, Marsh Wall London E14 (Tel: (01) 538 8860, or (01) 895 1229). Or you can contact the SIB Central Register which covers all authorised business: 3 Royal Exchange Buildings, London EC3V 3NL (Tel: (01) 929 3652).

Direct or through agents?

You do not save money by going directly through companies rather than agents. Generally, all that happens if you go directly to a company is that it saves the commission it might have paid the agent. Since you never pay the commission directly but are charged indirectly, this has no measurable impact on what you pay up front.

But if you go through an agent then you must be clear what you are getting. If the middleman is an independent financial adviser then under the Financial Services Act he must give you the best advice possible. In other words, he cannot simply tell you to buy the policies of XYZ company only. He must look at your financial position, the type of policy you need and then advise you accordingly.

If, on the other hand, you are dealing with a company representative then he must also offer you 'best advice' but can only sell you the products of his particular company, however unsuitable it might be. In the past confusion has arisen because it was not exactly clear who was an independent financial adviser and who was a company representative. The new Act sets out to clarify the distinction. It also alleviates the confusion regarding the commission charged by brokers. This confusion was compounded by the fact that you do not actually pay a fee to the person you buy an insurance product from. If you use the services of a solicitor or an accountant at the end of the day you get a bill. You may not like it, but it is clear enough.

On the other hand, insurance intermediaries are paid by insurance companies through commission. The way this system operated led to the suspicion that a particular intermediary might recommend the product of a company which pays higher commission rather than the product of a company that pays less commission but might be more suitable. Under the law you can always ask an intermediary how much commission he is getting. But few people ever do this. However, as a result of the proposed changes to the Financial Services Act, intermediaries will have to publicly disclose, without prompting, what commission they are getting. But these changes will not come into force till 1990.

Other agencies

You can get insurance through building societies or banks but in both cases the Financial Services Act would apply. They could sell either their own insurance policies or act as independent financial advisers and guide you through a range of policies.

If you are a member of a certain profession such as the civil service, medicine, teaching or nursing or belong to certain trades unions you may obtain insurance at special rates. These rates are likely to be cheaper than those elsewhere because they have been negotiated as packages with the underwriting insurance company or syndicate. But you need to check that what they are offering is what you need and that the terms are better than those available through other schemes.

Similarly, larger firms of brokers have set up their own schemes to cover certain risks like works of art, boats, horses, house contents and travel. These can offer very attractive rates but here you need to find out how the claims system works and who would be responsible if a claim was made.

Who are you with?

It is very easy to be confused about the difference between a broker and an insurance company. A broker could have the name ABC Insurance Services and this may make you feel that you are dealing directly with the insurance company when ABC are brokers who are acting as go-between with an underwriting company to place your insurance. It is important to bear this distinction in mind, particularly if a dispute arises.

2 The simple legal framework

Insurance is a contract between the insurer who, in return for a sum of money called the **premium**, agrees to pay the insured a certain other sum of money or its equivalent in kind should a certain event happen. It is assumed that the event is contrary to an insured's financial interest and the money he receives is intended to compensate him.

Proposal forms

It is possible for such an agreement to be an oral one, but almost always, it is in the form of a written document. If you want to arrange insurance the first document you will have to deal with is the proposal form. This is a document often of several pages, sometimes with illustrations, on which you provide information to the insurance company about yourself and the type of insurance you are seeking. A proposal form does not contain a **policy document** but a policy document may contain a proposal form. Before you complete the proposal form it is a good idea to read the policy document. You should complete the proposal form very carefully. The law requires that in a contract of insurance both you and the insurer must behave towards each other with utmost good faith.

What the forms consist of

Some of the questions on any proposal form are standard: name, address, occupation, including that of your spouse. If you have what is termed as a very high risk occupation and you are applying for **life insurance** or **permanent health insurance**, you may encounter difficulties in obtaining a desired policy. In motor car insurance the type of job you have will determine how much premium you pay. The proposal form is also likely to ask if you have tried getting this insurance before from another company and whether the company has turned you down. In recent years the **Insurance Ombudsman** has dealt with many complaints from people who find that they have been turned down more than once for an insurance policy and are branded as 'difficult to insure'. If you have been turned down it is best to state why because the circumstances may have changed and the reasons that lead to the refusal may no longer apply.

You may also be asked if an insurer has increased premiums or imposed special conditions, or even refused to renew a policy or cancelled it. There may be simple explanations for such things if they have happened to you. The insurer may have cancelled the policy because you have claimed too much, or you may be paying a higher premium because you live in a burglar-prone area. If your proposal is turned down it is not the end of the world, though it could prove inconvenient. One insurer's refusal to accept your proposal could be another's firm quotation. If you are dealing with a broker then he will be quite adept at hawking your proposal around – indeed he may have done so before he produces a proposal that suits you. The insurer is particularly interested in knowing the claims experience of you and your family. This will help him decide how much premium he should charge you.

When you have filled in the proposal form you have to make a **declaration** saying that the statements and answers made in connection with the proposal are true to the best of your knowledge and belief. Make sure that this is so and that you have not left out anything or misrepresented relevant information. In most cases, when you deal with a broker he or she is likely to fill in the proposal form but even then legally you have to make sure that when you sign the declaration you actually mean what you say. The declaration binds you in law to the information you have provided in the proposal. Also, what happens in practise is that you probably telephone your financial adviser asking for information about some insurance policy. He works out a rough calculation and sends you an **illustration** showing the premium to be paid, the benefits available and the proposal form.

A proposal form will state that you are under an obligation to disclose any material facts that affect your chances of procuring insurance. In simple terms, these are facts that make your situation different from other people's. In the classic case a person seeking a burglary policy was denied insurance when the insurance company discovered that some years previously he had had a criminal record. He had not disclosed this fact on the proposal form because it had not been requested. But the law held that this was a material fact that he should have disclosed even though he had not been specifically asked about it. If, after completing the proposal form and while the insurer is considering the proposal, facts change you are then required to disclose them. Again, at the time of renewal you must disclose material facts if they have changed since you took out the policy or since the last renewal. But in cases where renewal is automatic, such as long term life insurance, no such disclosure is required and you could happily pay your premium on your death bed without telling the insurance company of your imminent death.

A proposal is not a policy. Indeed, most proposal forms have a declaration in bold print saying something like, 'the liability of the insurer does not commence until the proposal has been accepted and the first premium paid'. So completing and signing a proposal form commits you to nothing and there is nothing to stop you completing several proposal forms. It is only when you say yes to a firm quotation and pay the first premium that you have a contract.

If, having paid the premium you find on reading the policy that you do not want to go through with it you can still get out. If you react quickly then you could get your money back less a charge for the time when the insurers were actually covering you. Some insurers will let you have the policy on approval for 14 days. Again, the Financial Services Act provides for a **cooling-off** period for investment business. If circumstances change after that and you find you can no longer sustain the policy then you can probably get out by paying what is known as a 'time on risk' charge. So for two months' cover you may be charged 25% of the annual premium, going up progressively to 50% of the annual premium on five months' cover. In the second or subsequent year you may be allowed a *pro rata* refund as renewing a policy is less expensive than issuing a new one. It is better to suspend a motor insurance policy rather than cancel, more so if you are expecting to buy another car soon. However, this advice applies to general insurance policies. If, for whatever reason, you surrender a life insurance policy then matters are more complicated and we enter the field of surrender values which will be dealt with when we discuss life insurance.

The proposal form from an insurance company is an incentive to encourage you to sample their products. It often includes a great deal of explanatory information. A policy document, on the other hand, is the legal document that expresses the contract you have entered into with the insurance company. It is an altogether more precise, legalistic document.

Policy documents

The policy comes along with a schedule. The policy by its nature is a generalised document. Nearly always printed, it covers the whole field of that particular type of insurance, be it motor cars or buildings. The schedule to the policy is your personalised policy. They both go together but the schedule which will have your name, address, policy number, indicates what parts of the policy apply to you. Thus, the policy may seem to cover you for items you do not have to insure and do not even possess. Fear not, for if you read the policy together with the schedule and mark the exemptions mentioned in the schedule you will realise just what you are covered for. If for some reason the schedule and the policy clash then the schedule will take precedence.

Since the policy is a legal document the wording of the policy is crucial. Case law has established that words will be given their plain, ordinary and popular meaning but where technical or legal words are used they will be given their technical (or legal) meaning. A phrase is considered as a whole and in its context. Thus, if the policy says it covers you for a list of perils including 'all other perils' the term includes only perils similar in kind to those listed. If for some reason there is ambiguity, then since the insurer has drawn up the policy, the meaning less favourable to him will be accepted.

The type of policy you have will depend on the type of insurance cover you need. But nearly all policies indicate: the sum insured or the limit of the indemnity, the geographical limits of the policy, a list of **conditions**, ie, how soon must you make the **claim**, **rights of cancellation**, details of arbitration clause and a list of **exclusions**.

Renewing your contract

Apart from life and health insurance, contracts run for a year before they have to be renewed. This is an occasion for you to shop around and decide how good the service of the existing insurer has been and whether you can get better service at a cheaper price. More likely, if you have gone through a broker for general insurance he might come up with a couple of alternative names suggesting that in the changed market climate they are now providing the better service. The insurers are at liberty to reject you but you can reject them as well, even after completing a proposal form. If you reject them you are under no obligation to do anything. Once you do not renew the policy lapses.

Most insurance companies offer a period of grace, anything between 15 to 30 days after the **renewal date** to enable you to renew the policy. If you pay your premium by the period of grace then your cover extends over that period. This is done either by extending the old policy, so any loss during that period will be covered by the old policy, or it allows the new premium to be paid so that the new policy takes over. It is not common to allow days of grace for payment of motor insurance policy but the renewal notice allows an extension of cover for 14 days in respect of the liabilities incurred by the **Road Traffic Acts**. If the premium has not been paid by the renewal date and an accident occurs within the ensuing 14 days, the insurer's liability will be limited to the cover specified in the renewal notice.

Insurance contracts have been described as wagering contracts in the sense that both depend on the happening of an event which is uncertain. The difference is that insurance contracts are enforceable in law whereas wagering contracts are not. Also, for an insurance contract to be valid there must be an '**insurable interest**'. In the early 18th century as life insurance was developing it became entangled with gambling. People would take out insurance on the lives of prominent men and women and important events in war and even on how long Louis XV's latest mistress would last. In 1708 parliament stopped all wagering on war and in 1774 parliament decreed that a life insurance contract was not valid 'except in cases where the person insuring shall have an interest in the life and death of the person insured.' A grown son maintaining an aged father has no insurable interest in the life of his father, but a child being maintained by his parents has an insurable interest in their lives.

Claiming insurance

The insurance company must pay any **claim** under a policy as soon as the amount has been ascertained. However, the policy may state that you have to make the claim within a certain time, or that the first £50 of the claim will have to be met by you, the insured. This is known as making an **excess payment** and is a common feature of most motor insurance policies. The loss may exceed the sum insured in which case you will not be able to recover all that you have lost.

Success of a claim may depend on proximate causes. English law holds these as more important than remoter causes. A personal accident policy may exclude a person from claiming if he has exposed himself to obvious risk of injury. In such circumstances if you try and cross a railway line in front of a train and are knocked down and killed the policy will not entertain the claim. But, if as a result of an accident you fall under a train then the claim could be met.

Instead of money, the claim can be met by the insurer offering to reinstate. This often applies to property but the insurance company that is compelled to reinstate as under the The Fires Prevention (Metropolis) Act 1774 cannot be compelled to reinstate more than the amount insured. However, if the insurance company agrees on its own to reinstate then once having agreed it cannot limit its liability to the sum insured, even if the reinstatement costs more than the company expected, or proves impossible.

3 Insurance – Who Needs it!

There are many people who think that insurance is either a waste of money or something that only the very rich need to concern themselves with. They probably have house insurance because their mortgage company insisted upon it but as this was all tied up at the time of getting the mortgage they may not even realise that they actually have this cover. Beyond that, life goes on and all is well – or is it?

The need for several types of insurance is perhaps best illustrated with a short story and to make it more interesting there is a quiz at the end of this chapter.

The Bowmans

Let's consider the story of everyday folk living in Oxbridge. Our story starts with Mr Bowman driving home along the winding country lanes leading to the new house that he and his wife have just bought. After a long day at the factory Mr Bowman was beginning to feel that he had more than earned the profits that he was likely to have made from today's business.

As today was the last day before he started his family holiday he had briefed his production manager and employees on what was expected of them while he was away. With over 40 years in the business, he knew he had no worries about his production manager other than the fact that he relied upon his technical knowledge a great deal. Business was booming and there was great demand for his new range of ladies' cosmetics.

Once home, Mr Bowman could see that his wife had done most of the holiday packing. So he busied himself with making sure that all the windows were properly fastened and the main water stopcock turned off. At that point, Mrs Boeman came home having delivered the family dog to the kennels. She had remembered to cancel her husband's squash match even though it had been an important league game. She had also remembered to cancel her daughter's cello lesson but was not quite sure what to do with their newly acquired sports equipment and musical instruments whilst they were on holiday.

Mrs Bowman knew that she had been very lucky to prise her husband away from his business for two whole weeks and wondered how long it would before he would bring their son into the business so that she and her husband could start taking it easy and look forward to fully retiring. Meanwhile, she hoped that nothing would happen to her husband or the business which would in any way jeopardise the comfortable lifestyle they had come to enjoy.

Mrs Bowman's day had not been entirely successful. The village fête had been a complete wash-out even though the thunderstorm had only lasted for half an hour just before the fête started. However, sunny Rumania awaited them and whilst Mr Bowman was hitching the caravan to the car Mrs Bowman looked forward to their holiday, although, at the back of her mind there was a slight niggle that they hadn't quite covered everything.

The quiz

As we can see from the above story, the Bowmans are a fairly typical family with two children, the husband running his own small business and the wife running the family home. There are millions of families such as this in Britain today.

Looking back through the short story, how many situations can you see where there is some risk being taken (or at least a chance that something could go wrong) which ought really to be covered by some form of insurance? Will Master Bowman be able to take over the family business without it being completely taxed away? Is Mrs Bowman insured for driving Mr Bowman's car on holiday? . . . and in Rumania? Is the caravan insured along with the car automatically? And are driving insurance requirements in Rumania the same as in the UK?

Where would the business be if anything happened to the production manager? What will happen to the Bowmans' standard of living if anything happens to Mr Bowman? Can Mr Bowman afford to retire? Finally, despite the weather, need the village fête have been a financial wash-out?

There are many more risks tucked away in our everyday story as indeed there are many risks taken by us all everyday of our lives. But they need not necessarily result in bringing financial burden on top of an unfortunate turn of events, provided the correct insurance cover is taken out in advance.

Are *you* covered?

4 What can you insure?

Just about everything – provided there is a chance that the event will not happen. So you can insure against you or your wife having twins, rain ruining your school fête or against your dog being lost. But if an event is bound to happen then the insurance company is unlikely to take on the risk (except, of course, life insurance).

Therefore, you cannot insure a house against fire after the fire has started. You cannot insure your holiday against being cancelled because of strike if you know perfectly well that a strike had already been called or has started. Other losses like those caused by rust, corrosion, or normal wear which in insurance policies are called **'gradually operating causes'** cannot be insured. The logic behind this is that insurance companies are taking a risk when they insure you. When they insure your car, the risk they are taking is that you may be involved in an accident. If you are not they do not pay out and the money they have collected from you becomes part of their general fund contributing to other claims and to profits. If you have an accident then they have to pay out and this depletes their resources.

So, in this sense an insurance contract is like a poker game where insurance companies assess the chances of landing a winning hand. If they are wrong they have to recalculate the premiums next time. There is only one type of insurance which can be taken out even when the event is certain – that is a policy to ensure that when you die your dependants will receive a certain sum of money.

Why have insurance?

The general rule of insurance is that you either need to have it because the law says so, or because it buys you peace of mind. Thus the law says you cannot drive a car without insurance. The Road Traffic Act 1972 lays down that you must have insurance to cover injury that you may cause to people. You must not allow others to drive your car or motor cycle unless your policy covers them or they have insurance of their own. In 1988 cover was extended to include damage to other people's property. In strict law the only motor insurance you require is **third party insurance**, you and the insurance company being the first two parties. The third party could be a passenger in your car, a pedestrian or someone in another car.

But for peace of mind nearly all motorists have policies that give them more cover than that. They either have a third party, fire and theft policy which includes liability for injury to other people, damage to their property and damage to, or loss of, your car or motor cycle by fire or theft. Many also have **comprehensive insurance** which, in addition, covers against accidental damage to your own car or motor cycle.

Most motor insurance policies cover you while you are driving someone else's car – but only for your liability to third parties. So if you are driving another person's car either he ought to have comprehensive policy which allows 'any driver' to drive the car – or your own policy must allow you to drive any car. Otherwise you could end up with a big bill should you damage his car.

Basically, there are two broad types of insurance: **life insurance** and **general insurance**. With life insurance you pay a premium to receive an income when you reach a given age or your heirs receive a certain sum of money if you die. Premiums are either paid regularly for a fixed number of years or perhaps for the whole of your life.

General insurance

General insurance, except when required by law, may be called essentially peace of mind insurance. You pay a premium, usually on a year's cover, to protect you against something happening – for example, your car being smashed up.

Household insurance

Household insurance is a popular form of general insurance and consists of two basic types: building insurance and contents insurance. Building insurance protects your house or flat against perils like the walls falling in, or the roof caving in, or fire. The law does not say you have to insure your home. But like most people you are probably borrowing money from a building society or bank to buy your home and they will insist you have the building insured. Make sure it is for the right amount. In the insurance trade this is known as the '**sum insured**'.

Contents insurance covers most movable items in your home: furniture, hi-fi, clothes, television, fridges, freezers, jewellery and sports equipment. You can have a **new-for-old contents policy** which means the insurance company will replace damaged goods with new ones. Or you may have **indemnity cover** where you will only be paid the value of the goods at the time of the loss or damage. Contents insurance covers a range of possessions but all sorts of other items can be added including, for example, loss of frozen food through a breakdown of a freezer, or the risk of your bicycle being stolen, **all risks insurance** and cover against accidental damage.

Other types of general insurance include:

Holiday insurance

This is to protect you against mishap. If you are injured while on holiday or fall ill you could face heavy bills. Holiday insurance can cover you for that. If your luggage is stolen or you lose money holiday insurance can meet the claims. If you have to cancel your holiday because of family illness or because of a strike, holiday insurance can compensate you.

Liability insurance

You could, in the course of work or just going about your business, cause damage to other people or their property. Liability insurance covers payments you may have to make to someone else because you have been careless and found to be legally liable for the damage caused.

Personal accident insurance

This pays money either weekly or in a lump sum to help you cope with ensuing financial problems.

Loan protection policy

If you borrow money and then cannot pay it back through sickness or accident, or redundancy, then you can use a loan protection policy to help you repay the loan.

Contact lens insurance

This covers loss or damage.

Pets insurance

If you have incurred expensive vet bills due to your animal needing treatment or if your pet is lost, stolen or dies, pet insurance can compensate you. This form of insurance cover also protects you if your pet's actions, through your carelessness, cause damage.

Pluvius insurance

This provides cover during certain occasions, for example, you may organise a school fête and it rains. Pluvius insurance will compensate for, say, the gate money and other items you may have lost because of the rain.

Thus, as you can see, there is an insurance cover available for almost anything. It is probably not a good idea to try and insure against everything since this would incur considerable expense. But from this wide choice insurance offers you protection in many areas. Some of them you need because the law says so, others will remove doubt and uncertainty about what might happen.

Now we shall look in more detail at the various kinds of insurance cover available.

5 Insurance for the home owner

As a house owner you are not legally required to insure anything. But this is where we enter the area of unwritten law. You are very likely to have borrowed money from a bank or building society to buy your home. They have lent money to you against the security of the house or flat and are, almost certainly, going to require that you insure your home against fire and other possible calamities. Again, while there is nothing in the law which says you should insure your furniture, your clothes, television, video sets and valuables you would be extremely foolish not to do so. So **household contents insurance** is something you will need. The type and range of household insurance will depend on whether you own a house or a flat. A flat presents certain complications which we shall look at later. Here, let us concentrate on the broad principles of house insurance.

The basic bricks of household insurance

Bricks is precisely what house insurance covers you for. It is an insurance for the building which protects you against fire and a number of specified perils. It is important to remember that anything not listed will not be covered. Most policies will list the following:

Fire

If you deliberately set the place alight you are unlikely to be able to claim but otherwise this section of the policy has no specific exclusions. However, it does not normally cover smoke damage which you either have to ask for or go to one of the few insurers that give all risks cover on building insurance. You can also get cover for explosion, lightning, earthquakes and thunderbolts.

Theft, or attempted theft

The insurer will cover you for anything under the **Theft Act**, although not in Scotland where the Act does not apply. But insurers tend not to provide cover if the house was unoccupied when the burglary or attempted break-in took place. Normally, 'unoccupied' means a period of 30 days or more when the house is not lived in. However as the crime rate has gone up, particularly in London, you will find insurers looking at the meaning of 'unoccupied' rather more closely. This will affect you particularly if you live in an area which is considered 'higher risk' by the insurance company. In such an area, if nobody is at home during the day because both you and your partner are working you may find it difficult to get an insurance company to take on the risk. If they do take on the risk they may charge a lot more. Insurers will look carefully at the security you have: five-lever mortice deadlock on the final door of exit and key-operated locks on all ground-floor windows, for example.

If you have a **second home** and this is likely to be unoccupied for considerable periods then again you may be paying more for insurance. But second homes, as a general rule, are not in high risk crime areas, so insurance cover is not difficult to obtain.

Subsidence, landslip or heave of the site on which the building stands

You can even have avalanche cover under this clause but there are quite a few things not covered: damage caused by coastal or river bank erosion, by the demolition of a building, or by structural alteration or structural repair, or if the damage is due to faulty workmanship or the use of defective materials. You are also likely to find that the policy does not cover damage to your swimming pool, hard courts, walls, patios, drives, paths, gates, fences, hedges or external service tank unless during the subsidence or landlsip or heave, the building was damaged as well. You may find that under this section you are paying quite a high excess, up to 3% or 5% of the current cost of completely rebuilding your home.

Storm, tempest, flood

This relates to a family of cover that comes under the broader title of water and impact damage. Certain general principles apply to this sort of insurance. The first £25 or even up to the first £100 of every claim is likely to be excluded. As far as storm damage is concerned frost is not covered although 'storm' can include hailstones and other adverse weather conditions. You are unlikely to be covered for damage to gates, walls, fences, hedges or for subsidence, heave or landslip. The logic behind this is that the insurance company will cover you for any abnormal weather conditions but not for damage caused by the fact that you have not maintained your property properly or because over time roofs, etc have deteriorated. As one judge said, 'one gust does not a storm make', and the policy is meant to cover you for many gusts of an unusual kind, such as the one we saw in the south of England during October 1987.

Leaks and spills

You can be covered for leakage of oil from any storage tank, pipe, fixed heating installation or other apparatus. You are also covered if water overflows or escapes from water tanks or apparatus or pipes. Most modern policies specify that by 'apparatus' they mean fixed domestic heating or water installations, plumbed-in washing machines or dishwashers, aquaria and water beds. The point to check is whether the damage to the pipes themselves or the containers is covered. Some policies whilst paying out on the damage caused by water or oil escaping, baulk at paying out for the pipes or containers.

What you get on a claim under this section may be affected

by an **excess clause** which means that you have to meet the first £10 or £20 of the damage and, of course, insurance companies may deny the claim if the house was unoccupied.

Frost

Coping with Jack Frost is rather difficult. Frost, as the **insurance ombudsman** notes, is not one of the insured perils listed under a normal household policy. Frost damage to pipes or tanks is covered and the 'water overflowing' section may include wording such as 'freezing of water tanks, apparatus or pipes' and that may cover the situation. But this is a cover you may have to look for as it does not feature in all policies. Even if it does it will come with a long list of exclusions such as tennis courts, swimming pools, drives, paths, gates, fences, hedges etc, or if the buildings are unoccupied. You may have to meet an excess of the order of £20 to £30.

Impact damage

Here policies vary quite dramatically. In some you are only covered for impact damage by any vehicle or animal, in others you are covered for falling trees, telegraph poles, lamp-posts, aircraft and trains. But while the policy will help you repair the house if a tree has fallen on it, it may not pay for the cost of felling any remaining parts of the tree or removing the tree. Then again, if while you are parking your car in the garage you hit it or the house, or do not have your brakes on and the car rolls on and demolishes part of your wall then you may find that you have to bear the excess.

Riot and civil commotion

Three persons may not only be a crowd, they can also cause a riot. We often use the word loosely but when it comes to insurance it has a precise meaning. Legally, a riot must involve three persons, they must have a common purpose, they must assemble with the intention of helping each other, and their common purpose must be carried out with force or a show of force which would alarm a reasonable person. A civil commotion is something between a riot and a civil war.

If such circumstances apply and your property has suffered damage you need to make your claim quickly.

Under the Riot (Damages) Act the money insurers pay out can be reclaimed from the government in seven days, so if you are making a claim under this clause, make it quickly. **Malicious damage** also comes under this heading and will cover you for damage by malicious persons or vandals. As in riot, the policy will require you to inform the police as soon as possible about any loss or damage. Some policies are more restrictive than others and will only pay if the damage is caused by somebody acting on behalf of a political party or during a political disturbance. If you or your tenants cause the damage you cannot hope to claim, nor can you do so if the house is unoccupied.

Aircraft

You can be covered if an aircraft lands on your house, or some aerial device or article drops from the aircraft on to your building. But you are not likely to be covered if, as Concorde passes overhead, the resulting sonic boom damages your home.

Accidental damage

This can cover damage to a host of things ranging from wash basins, pedestals, sinks, bidets, lavatory pans, shower trays and what is generally understood as sanitary fixtures. You can also be covered for pipes and cables for which you are legally responsible.

If you splash ink all over the wall paper or put your foot through the ceiling, provided you have not done it deliberately your policy should cover you for it. Such damage generally comes under the heading of any accident or misfortune option though you may pay higher premium for such cover and have to pay for the excess. This section also excludes quite a few things you cannot claim for: if the workmanship is faulty, if defective design or defective materials have been used, or there is shrinkage or expansion by wet or dry rot.

Other losses

A building insurance policy should also cover the rent you may lose if you are the landlord of the building and damage to it means you are losing out on rent. If, as an owner-occupier you have to seek alternative accommodation because damage to your house means you cannot live there then you should be able to claim for the cost of comparable accommodation. But usually there is a limit to such a claim, something like 10% of the building sum insured. Of course, you cannot stay in the alternative accommodation for ever, only for as long as it takes to make your house fit for habitation.

Fees

The policy should also help you meet architects', surveyors', consultants' and legal fees which may be incurred in rebuilding or repairing the building, or removing debris, and should cover any additional costs to meet your obligations under local by-laws.

Flats

If you own a flat then the building insurance you need will be somewhat different in nature. A flat, whether it be conversion of a house into a number of flats or a block of flats, will have some common parts. The lease will specify how these common parts are to be insured.

If, as is very often the case, you are buying a flat with a loan from a building society or a bank they are likely to insist that you have an insurance to cover your flat and the common areas. The two insurances are likely to run parallel with low premiums paid for the common insurance and quite high premiums paid for the main flat insurance. The problem arises when the loan on the flat is repaid and you do not remember to keep up the cover on the common part. If you do not, you could suddenly find you are underinsured. Some owners of flats on a long lease club together and insure all the flats as a block and divide the premium amongst the flat owners.

More common in modern leases is for the leasor to be responsible for the insurance of the building, including the common parts and the individual flats, under one central policy. The premium is then divided between the individual flat owners and usually paid through the service charge. In some leases the landlord is responsible for the common parts, with the individual flat owner responsible for his or her own flat. This can be tricky. For instance, if there is a burglary the landlord will pay for the replacement of the front door since this is held to be part of the common parts but any loss of contents will be your responsibility. He will, however, be responsible for any damage to your flat as a result of burst pipes, etc. However, if a calamity should occur and the flat below is underinsured, you will find it difficult to rebuild. So look carefully at any such arrangement.

House contents insurance

You can have the contents of your house insured together with the building insurance or separately. You do not have to go through the same insurers for both but when making a claim you may find things easier if you do. Contents insurance is exactly how we would understand the term – the contents in your home including **money**.

There are two basic types of contents insurance: **specified perils** or **all risks**. In many respects contents insurance covers many of the specified perils we have just been looking at under building insurance. This makes the policy easy for the insurer to write and, in many ways, easy for you to understand the cover being provided. All risks policy, in theory, insures against all contingencies, except the ones that are excluded. The problem is that the exclusions can be as long as your arm and nearly always contain an exclusion for mechanical and electrical breakdown. So if a fire was caused by the breakdown of an electric insulation, an all risks policy would not cover the damage. But a specified perils policy would provide cover.

The sections of a household contents policy listing specified perils are very similar to building insurance:

Fire

The usual cover, but if you scorch your clothes while ironing, or your oil heater is faulty and fills the room with dense greasy smoke that ruins your clothes, walls, curtains and if this damage has not been accompanied by flames you will not be able to claim on this insurance unless the policy says so. Here an all risks policy has an advantage since it covers damage from smoke.

Water and impact damage

Much the same situation as buildings insurance but in the past some policies contained a clause that if the premises had been **unoccupied** for a period of time, usually 30 days, water had to be turned off at the mains and all pipes and systems drained. The advent of central heating and the need to keep it on to prevent freezing has made this exclusion somewhat redundant. In the case of impact damage the policy is slightly less restrictive than in building insurance. You can be covered for the cost of removing the object that fell on your house provided the damage this caused to your house is accepted.

Riot and civil commotion

Very similar to building insurance clauses.

Theft

Here, should you make a claim the insurance company is likely to quiz you about how it happened. Were you deceived? Did you fall for the old classic story of the man supposedly in the antique business who says: 'I'll just take it to the car and have a look in the book to give you the right price', and then vanishes? If so, you may not be able to claim compensation. On the other hand, if a person claims to have come to read the meter and then uses the opportunity to steal, you could claim that he used deception to enter. Normally, if there has been theft of money you will not be able to claim unless force has been used. But, if for whatever reason you allow a thief in your home, and then accidentally shut him in and he steals money and breaks out, you can claim. If a house or flat is wholly or partly let then loss is excluded unless force is used to enter the premises or leave them. Theft is also excluded while the house is **unfurnished** or **unoccupied**.

Accidental damage

This covers a wide field, for example, accidental damage to television, radio, recording and audio equipment. Normally, under such insurance cover the type of damage is not made clear but there is usually a limit on the amount that can be claimed and portable items are not included. Moreover, you cannot claim for items that have suffered normal wear and tear, or where there has been electronic, or mechanical breakdown. Depending on the policy you may not be covered for accidental breakage of fixed glass in furniture, mirrors, etc.

You can also have an optional extra accidental damage to valuables or all risks cover. This would cover you for paint spilling onto a carpet, smoke damage and scorching. But such policies have exclusions which you should look out for. Just because you have accidentally wound the clock up a bit too much and damaged it in the process does not mean that you can claim for the clock.

Television and radio masts and aerials

This shows an interesting co-relation between buildings insurance and contents insurance. Contents insurance will cover you for a damaged aerial. But if a damaged aerial falls down and on the way it causes other damage then that will be covered by building insurance.

What about items taken outside the house?

Usually, possessions that you take outside are covered, as are items that always stay in the open – but this does not include trees, plants or your garden gnome. But look under the special insurance section to see how you can cover your garden gnome. There is often a limit to what is paid for loss or damage to things outside the home and an excess of anything up to £25 may have to be met.

What if the property is elsewhere?

If your belongings are not at home they are still covered. So your children's possessions at school or college are covered although college students can also obtain a special policy. If you or a member of your family loses possessions from a building where you work this will be compensated. But in a building other than your office, theft would be covered only if **force** was used to enter or leave the building. If your clothes have been ruined by heavy rain as you were leaving the office you are unlikely to be able to claim unless that rain was part of a storm or a flood.

If you have removed your furniture to a furniture depository for sale or exhibition you may not be covered but you can be if you have them in a bank or safe deposit box – even if they are stolen while on their way there or back. Under some policies you can cover contents as they are being moved permanently to another home.

What happens if you borrow someone else's possessions?

If you borrow your friend's golf clubs and then they are stolen you cannot claim on your policy. The reason for this is that you had **no insurable interest** in the golf clubs and could not expect to be indemnified. It is your friend's responsibility to ensure that the golf clubs were insured and inform the company of the loan.

Insuring the food in your freezer

Depending on the insurance company cover for food in a freezer is either an optional extra or something that is thrown in for free. However, should the electricity supply to your freezer be cut due to a strike by the electricity authorities, and your food goes bad, then you may not be covered. You may have to take out a special Lloyd's policy in order to claim compensation for this. Deterioration in the food due to breakdown is covered but this depends on how old your freezer is. The point to consider is – do you need extra cover for food in the freezer? If a storm cuts electricity supply or a burglar breaks in then you may be covered as part of your general policy in any case.

Money

Cover for loss of money depends on how the policy defines money. We all know when we have money but money in this context has a multitude of meanings depending on the policy. For example, 'personal money' can mean cheques, postal orders, stamps, travel tickets, travellers cheques, premium bonds, even credit cards. However money is defined, it is covered under a contents policy for the usual specified perils but if it is lost outside the home, then the cover may be limited to the money lost when there was forcible entry or exit from the building.

There are various other extensions you can have under this type of policy like insuring bicycles, sports goods, etc but we shall look at these separately.

All risks insurance

This does not quite mean that every risk under the sun is covered but it will cover you for all the specified perils (subject to exclusions) accidental damage and unexplained loss. You pay as much as 25% or more for the cover and on almost every claim you will have to meet the excess.

There are various ways you can get an all risks insurance. It may be obtained as an extension of contents policy, or separately, although this is not very popular with insurers who have found that on such policies they have paid out rather a lot of money.

Unspecified personal effects

Personal effects is not defined and the way this insurance cover works is that the policy specifies the items that do *not* fall into this category. Such exclusions will vary with insurers but all of them will require that you state that the sum insured represents the maximum total value of those items which you and your family may have on you or with you when outside the home. Underinsurance could be disastrous. You can include the possessions of all those family members who live with you permanently. If you want cover outside the UK you can get it worldwide for 30 or 60 days in a year. More extensive worldwide cover will mean an extension of the policy. The policy normally specifies the maximum to be paid for each article, which is approximately £200.

Unspecified valuables

This overlaps with personal effects but normally means cameras, binoculars and other such objects. The difference is that the limit for each unspecified valuable is almost double that of personal effects at around £500. You are not expected to have the pieces valued individually or provide proof of values but if you make a claim you may have to produce evidence of value.

Specified valuables

You can also insure specified valuables such as **jewellery**, small curios, stamp or coin collections, pictures, expensive cameras, etc. Insurers require that you specify pieces of equipment such as electric typewriters, domestic sewing machines, musical instruments, hi-fi equipment, portable televisions. Items have to be listed individually with a separate value for each. For those that are over a set figure, a valuation or receipt must be produced to the insurers when taking out the insurance. The main difficulty arises with jewellery and it may be advisable to consult the **Incorporated Society of Valuers and Auctioneers (ISVA)** who would provide a list of their members to do the valuation for you. The premium rates will depend on where you live and how high the risk of theft is in that area.

Musical instruments

Your household contents policy should cover musical instruments but you may find that this is for a limited amount and only if the damage is done by perils listed in the policy. Musical instruments can be easily stolen since most of them are compact enough to be picked up and carried away. They can also be easily damaged and the cost of replacing some of them could run into thousands of pounds.

To make sure you are fully protected you should have the instruments listed as **specified valuable** under an **all risks** schedule. Without this under normal household contents policy you will only be covered for accidents and benefits from home. Adding all risks cover to a home contents policy costs £1.50 per £100 insured. So if your particular instrument is worth less than, say, £500 it will be covered under the heading of personal possessions.

Some insurers issue special policies to cover musical instruments on an all risks basis. But such policies have a great many exclusions such as the breaking of strings or reeds, effects of climate and an unattended instrument in a vehicle. Under some policies you can insure for each type of instrument individually, others merely differentiate between classical and electrical equipment. You will get replacement value but as policies are not index-linked it is worth reviewing the cover regularly. Premium rates vary for individual instruments but rates decrease the higher the cover.

However, those making a living from playing musical instruments may find the situation rather complicated. The insurance industry has no great love for entertainers. They regard them as a bad risk even for household cover on the grounds that they spend a lot of their time away from home, especially in the evening. So the chances of being burgled are vastly increased. Moreover, there are a number of young people who do not have household policies which means they cannot simply extend them to cover musical instruments. The answer would be the **specialist policy** we have discussed.

How much should you insure for?

As a general rule it is possible for most people to *overinsure* their house, but *underinsure* the contents of their home.

The sum your home is insured for is the amount of money for which your home is covered and is the most your insurer will pay under any circumstances. This sum must be adequate and since most policies specify the amount to be paid, if there is underinsurance you may find that your claim is not met in full.

The problem is that when it comes to insuring your home you are likely to take the market value of your home as a guide. That, as the **Association of British Insurers (ABI)** says, is not a reliable guide. You should calculate on the basis of the full **rebuilding cost** of your home to make sure that you are covered for the right amount – neither too much nor too little. If you are covered for too little the risks are obvious; if you are covered for too much you are wasting money.

What should the rebuilding cost include?

The rebuilding cost should include an allowance for permanent fittings, such as central heating and additional charges which could be involved in rebuilding – demolition costs, professional fees and the requirements of local authorities. You must also add on an amount to take care of garages, fences, gates, paths and swimming pools. It is a good idea to get expert help in arriving at the figure you should be insured for. However, the ABI publish a guide about how to make the calculations (see chart titled 'How much would it cost to rebuild your home?' on pages 42–43).

However, this cannot suit all purposes. If you have a three storey house, for instance, you ought to follow an alternative route. First, find out the external floor area of your home – both upstairs and downstairs. The best way to do this is go outside and measure the length and breadth of your home and multiply these figures. If you have a terraced house then you will have to measure inside and then add the thickness of the walls. If you have an integral garage it should be included in the calculation, but if the garage is separate or built on the side of the house you should add an appropriate amount later.

Now that you know the ground floor area it may be possible to simply double the figure, but the upper floors may be of a different size. In that case you will have to measure them separately. If there is a third storey add three quarters of the area of the third storey. Insert the answer against A.

Then, identifying your type of home and area, use the chart to find the correct age bracket and, according to whether your house is small, medium or large, choose the appropriate figure per square foot. This is figure B. Multiply A and B. To this figure add rebuilding costs for a garage which, if they are not an integral part of the house, range from £2,150 for single prefabricated garages to £7,400 for a double detached in brick, and complete the calculation.

You may find that when you have done this your house is actually overinsured. The reason for that is the tremendous boom in house prices which is causing all sorts of problems. For a start, it is leading to distortions. There can be large variations in prices not only between similar houses in different parts of the country, but also in different parts of the same town. For instance, one house may overlook the river and the other the gas works. The prices of the two houses will be very different, but the rebuilding costs won't vary that much.

The rebuilding cost of a post-war semi-detached house in London is £54,500 and in Yorkshire it is £42,500. Yet the Londoner is probably insuring his semi-detached for an average of £92,000, while the Yorkshireman is insuring his for £26,000. The Londoner is overinsured, the Yorkshireman is underinsured and could be badly out of pocket should his house be burnt down. While the rapid inflation in the south of England had made us a two-nation country, in a rather curious way the cost of building homes in the north is not that much different from the prosperous south.

The overinsurance is crucial for since the storm damage of October 1987 rates for house insurance have gone up from about £1.80 per every £1,000 of cover to something nearer to £2 which means cover for a house insured for £40,000 costs in the region of £80 as opposed to £70 before the storm. So, overinsurance could be expensive.

But against this must be set the possibility that we are likely to be quite a bit underinsured in home contents policy. Here we are always buying new things but we do not always increase contents insurance. Nor is the building insurance altered when a new kitchen is fitted or a patio extension made.

House insurance–a guide

How much would it cost to re-build your home?

SEPTEMBER 1987 costings — £ per square foot (external)

		PRE 1920			1920–1945			1946–DATE		
		LARGE	MEDIUM	SMALL	LARGE	MEDIUM	SMALL	LARGE	MEDIUM	SMALL
DETACHED HOUSE	Region 1	56.50	61.50	60.00	54.00	56.50	57.00	46.00	49.00	49.00
	2	51.50	56.00	54.50	49.50	51.50	51.50	42.00	44.50	44.50
	3	46.50	50.50	49.00	44.50	46.00	46.50	37.50	40.00	40.00
	4	44.00	47.50	46.50	42.00	43.50	44.00	35.50	38.00	38.00
	Typical Area ft²	3450	1700	1300	2550	1350	1050	2550	1350	1050
SEMI-DETACHED HOUSE	Region 1	55.50	56.50	56.50	58.50	56.50	56.50	42.00	44.50	47.50
	2	50.50	51.50	51.00	53.50	51.50	51.50	38.00	40.50	43.00
	3	45.50	46.00	46.00	48.00	46.50	46.00	34.50	36.50	39.00
	4	43.00	43.50	43.50	45.50	43.50	43.50	32.50	34.50	36.50
	Typical Area ft²	2300	1650	1200	1350	1150	900	1650	1350	1050
DETACHED BUNGALOW	Region 1	The chart does not cover pre-1920 bungalows, as few such properties were built.			58.50	54.50	55.50	50.00	50.50	52.50
	2				53.00	49.50	50.50	45.50	46.00	47.50
	3				48.00	44.50	45.50	41.00	41.00	43.00
	4				45.00	42.00	43.00	38.50	39.00	40.50
	Typical Area ft²				1650	1400	1000	2500	1350	1000
SEMI-DETACHED BUNGALOW	Region 1				60.50	61.50	54.00	49.00	49.00	51.00
	2				55.00	56.00	49.00	44.50	44.50	46.50
	3				49.50	50.50	44.00	40.00	40.00	41.50
	4				47.00	47.50	42.00	37.50	38.00	39.50
	Typical Area ft²				1350	1200	800	1350	1200	800
TERRACED HOUSE	Region 1	60.00	59.00	58.50	58.50	58.50	58.00	42.00	45.50	50.50
	2	54.50	53.50	53.50	53.50	53.00	52.50	38.50	41.50	46.00
	3	49.00	48.00	48.00	48.00	48.00	47.50	34.50	37.50	41.50
	4	46.50	45.50	45.50	45.50	45.00	44.50	32.50	35.00	39.00
	Typical Area ft²	1650	1350	1050	1350	1050	850	1650	1300	900

Regions

1. London Boroughs and Channel Islands
2. South East
   Bedfordshire, Berkshire, Buckinghamshire, Essex, Hampshire, Hertfordshire, Kent, Oxfordshire, Surrey, East Sussex, West Sussex.
3. North West, South West, East Anglia and Scotland
   Cheshire, Greater Manchester, Lancashire, Merseyside, Avon, Cornwall, Devon, Dorset, Gloucestershire, Somerset, Wiltshire, Cambridgeshire, Norfolk, Suffolk and the whole of Scotland.
4. Northern, West Midlands, Wales, Yorkshire & Humberside, East Midlands and Northern Ireland.
   All other counties.

Source: Association of British Insurers

Total external area (upstairs and down)	=	______ sq. ft.	A
'Per-square-foot' rebuilding cost	=	£ ______	B
Multiply A×B	=	£ ______	C
Add for garage (see notes overleaf)	=	£ ______	D
Estimate the cost of rebuilding any outbuildings, walls and fences and any other items covered and put this figure against E.		£ ______	E
Now add C, D and E together	=	£ ______	
If your policy is not index-linked add on a suitable allowance for inflation		£ ______	
TOTAL	=	£ ______	

Calculating contents insurance

As we have seen, the basis for settlement of your claims will depend on whether you are insured for **indemnity** or **replacement as new**. If you insure on an indemnity basis you will be paid the cost of repairing damaged articles or of replacing what has been stolen or destroyed, less an amount for wear, tear and depreciation. For items covered on a replacement-as-new basis you will be paid the full cost of repairs if they are damaged or the cost of replacing them with equivalent new articles if they are stolen or destroyed. Furniture, domestic appliances, television, videos and audio equipment can normally be insured on replacement-as-new basis but not usually clothing and household linen.

In calculating what your insurance should be worth the guide prepared by the ABI can be very useful (see page 45). What you should do is list on the chart all the items to be insured. For this you need to go from room to room carefully estimating what it would cost to replace every item at today's prices. For clothing you should deduct for wear and tear – generally a suit is estimated to have a five-year life span, so for each year you have had your suit deduct one fifth of the price of an equivalent new suit at today's prices.

In order to keep the sum insured up to date you can have it **index-linked**. This simply means that your sum insured is automatically changed every month with any movement in the retail price index – there is no charge for any increase between renewal dates. But even if it is index-linked it is a good policy to increase the sum insured if you add to your possessions. Index-linking only works if your sum insured is right in the first place. You should also keep your bills and valuations since you are likely to need them in case of a claim.

Contents insurance – a guide

CHECK LIST	Lounge	Dining room	Kitchen	Hall, stairs,	Landing	Main bed-room	2nd bed-room	3rd bed-room	Bath-room/ Toilet	Garage & out-buildings	TOTALS
Carpets, rugs and floor coverings											
Furniture: tables, chairs, stools, suites, cabinets, sideboards, bookcases. Bedroom, bathroom and kitchen furniture											
Soft furnishings, curtains and their fittings, cushions											
Televisions, videos and audio equipment											
Household appliances: cooker, refrigerator/ freezer, washing machine, vacuum cleaner, electrical goods, heaters											
Cooking utensils and provisions, cutlery, china, glass, food, drink											
Valuables: gold and silver articles, jewellery, pictures, clocks, watches, cameras, ornaments, collections											
Leisure: sports equipment, cycles, books, records, tapes, musical instruments, toys											
Garden furniture, lawn-mower, ladders, tools, paint, fuel											
Household linen: bedding, towels, table linen											
Clothing											
Other items											

If your policy is not index-linked, add on a suitable allowance for inflation.
You may, of course, have other rooms and possessions not listed here.

TOTAL £

Allowance for inflation during year at .... %

Your contents should be insured for £

Source: Association of British Insurers

6 Insurance for the income earner

You have your health, you have your wealth and your future looks secure. But what happens if you fall ill and cannot work or, perhaps, decide that having worked hard all your life you would like to take it easy – retire and live near the beach? Or you die? How are you going to make sure that you will continue to have sufficient income for yourself and/or your family? This is where several types of insurance cover can help you plan for the future.

All these insurances come under the generic title of **life insurance**, though in many cases it would be more correct to call it death insurance since they often provide money to dependants of a person who has died. We shall also be looking at **health insurance**, though again it would be more correct to call it ill-health insurance since it is meant to provide an income when you are sick and cannot work. The best way to look at life insurance is to see it as a pendulum. At one end of the pendulum it provides protection to you if you fall ill or to your family if you die; at the other end it can provide you with investment benefits. In between there is a wide variety of products often with bewildering names. How you swing between the extremes of the pendulum depends on your needs and your financial situation.

Protection

If it is financial protection for your family that you are looking for in the event of your death, the simplest insurance is temporary or **term insurance**. It is also known as level term or protection only policy. It exists for a certain length of time, hence the expression term, and covers the risk of death within that period. Insurance companies are able to offer such policies at very cheap rates compared to other forms of life insurance since it is very possible that nothing will ever be paid out on the policy. If you die, they pay; if you live they don't!

In theory, you can insure your life or that of your spouse for any amount but if it is excessive in relation to your income this may cause suspicion and the insurance company may refuse it.

The cost of term insurance will depend on:

- Your age when you take out the insurance
- The length of time covered by the policy
- The options included in the policy, like extending the term or increasing the cover
- Whether the insurance company in question asks for a full medical or agrees on a policy without much medical examination
- Whether the insurance company is well known or a new one trying to break into the market.

Term insurance can be for very short periods. You may be a high-flyer changing jobs who has high life insurance cover in both your old job and your new one, but there may still be a gap of a few days when you do not have life cover. In such a situation you may decide to take out temporary life cover of a few days to cover for this period. Such cover is *not* cheap.

Insurance companies which have strict medicals tend to charge less for term insurance than those that have a rather prefunctory one. But if you go for a strict medical it is possible you may be refused insurance. Insurance companies keep a list of those who have been refused. With the Aids scare most companies now insist on fairly comprehensive medicals and so this distinction is not as great as was the case even a couple of years back.

Increasing term insurance

This is a type of term insurance where the amount payable on death gets higher as time goes by. So if you have taken out a 20-year policy then every five years the sum payable could increase. If death should occur within years one to five, your dependants may get £20,000; if death occurs between six to ten years, they may get £25,000 and so on. But again, with the onset of Aids such policies are more difficult to obtain. Generally, the premium remains the same over the 20-year policy period.

As a variation you can also have increasable term insurance where for more premiums you can increase the sum assured.

Decreasing term insurance

Here we have almost the exact opposite in that the cover provided decreases over a period of time. The most common use for such policies are for **mortgage protection**. The simple repayment mortgage consists of an interest payment plus a certain proportion of the capital. Over the years, the interest proportion of the payment decreases and the capital proportion increases. Building societies like borrowers to take out an insurance policy to cover the mortgage so that should he or she die, they can get their loan back and do not have to foreclose on a mortgage and probably be involved in unpleasant publicity.

The insurance policy has the same term as the mortgage policy and follows the same curve as the capital outstanding on the mortgage loan. The premium is generally averaged out to be the same throughout the period although some insurance companies will adjust their calculations so that premiums need not be paid in the last few years of the term. The policy remains valid and premiums must be paid even if the mortgage has been paid up. This can happen when you sell the house and buy another property but then the policy can be used to cover the mortgage on the new home. In such cases, however, care needs to be taken to make sure that the insurance cover is not out of line with the mortgage repayments being made.

This type of policy can also be used to provide cover if you are paying off a loan by instalments or building up a fund for a particular purpose. Should you die in mid-course the insurance policy could provide the remaining money to build up the fund.

Family income benefit

This is rather a clever variation of term insurance and one that is becoming popular. What happens is that if you die within the term of the insurance then a tax-free sum is paid for the remaining period of the term to your spouse. You could take out a policy where in the event of your death during the next 35 years your wife and children will get £10,000 a year. The policy would show the sum insured to be of £350,000 during the first year, £340,000 in the second year and £320,000 in the third and so on with each year decreasing the sum payable. The reason why the policy is expressed in capital sum is because when payments are made it is seen as repayment of capital so they do not attract income tax. The income will only be paid if you die within the next 35 years, or whatever the term of the policy is. The insurance company may also offer to pay a lump sum instead of the annual sum of £10,000.

There are variations on this policy with some insurance companies increasing both the cover and the premium at a predetermined rate, say 5% per annum in order to cope with inflation. But the more variation you have on such a policy, the more difficult it becomes to underwrite and the premium increases quite substantially. Such policies can also be used for **inheritance tax** purposes, particularly if both husband and wife were to die, leaving orphaned children. However, such policies would require the setting up of a **trust fund** and are quite complicated.

Convertible term insurance

This begins as a straight term policy which you can convert to **whole life** or **endowment** policies without a medical check or any questions raised about your occupation. Thus, a man aged 45 might want to buy £40,000 of cover at the lowest possible cost but wants to keep all his options open. He does not want to find out, say at 50, an age at which life companies tend to be particular about medical exminations, that he can no longer pass the medical and therefore buy endowment or whole life insurance.

Generally, the option to convert can be exercised at any time within the agreed term, although some companies specify that you can only convert every five years. Some policies also have an **increasibility option** where at specified intervals – three years or five years – you can increase the sum assured on the policy. However, do note that as a result of the Budget changes of March 1984 which removed **life assurance premium relief (LAPR)**, exercise of an option can mean varying the policy. This could mean that you will lose your tax relief on the premiums if the policy was taken out before 13 March, 1984.

Investment

The other swing of the pendulum is towards investment and permanent insurance policies basically cater for this need. A permanent insurance policy is a policy which does not expire at the end of a specified term. The sum assured will definitely be paid either on death or at the end of a specified period. There are various types of permanent insurance, but two broad categories: whole-life policies and endowment policies.

Whole life policies

A whole life policy guarantees to pay an agreed sum of money to your family should you die. You decide how much you want your family to receive, say £20,000. The life office then calculates the premium you must pay each year, taking into account the benefit you want, your age, health, and in some cases, the type of job you do.

This premium is then paid by you each year for the rest of your life. Or not quite the rest of your life. Life companies quote premium rates calculated on the assumption that no premium is payable after the age of 85. In practise some people who buy such insurance will stop paying premiums at the age of 60 or 65 so that all premiums are paid out of earned income. This practise started when life insurance premiums attracted tax relief. But although that has been abolished the practise continues. It does mean that such insurance costs a lot more than term insurance.

You can cash in these policies but you will not obtain a high return if you do so in the first few years. You must think carefully before taking out such a policy. If it is protection for the short term you are seeking, term insurance would be more advantageous. If investment is your aim then other investment mediums provide a better return. A policy like this can be useful in settling an **inheritance tax** bill but you must make sure that the proceeds go to your heirs otherwise it will be added to become part of your estate.

There is one type of whole life policy that may be useful, particularly for married women going back to work. Let us say you are in your forties and now that the children are at school you want to work again. You could then take out a whole life insurance on your husband's life. If you buy a with-profits or unit-linked policy you could stop paying premiums when you retire but the investment you have made will go on appreciating or if it is with profits, acquiring bonuses as long as your husband is alive. On his death you can draw a capital sum.

Endowment insurance

Endowment insurance is a combination of a savings plan and the protection that term insurance provides, but the protection element is so small that it really has little to do with life insurance. As its name implies, endowment insurance consists of two separate elements: pure endowment and decreasing term insurance. In the former, the premiums that you pay are rolled up at compound interest to produce a lump sum payable at the end of the period. At any point during this endowment period a certain capital sum will be built to your credit. The decreasing term insurance is enough to make up the pure endowment element of the sum assured.

If you buy a £20,000 non-profit endowment policy for a 30-year term then at the end of the term you will get £20,000. However, if you die within the first year of the policy then the premiums you have paid will not be enough to give your dependants £20,000 and then the pay-out will come from the term insurance element of the policy.

Your share of the profits

We have been talking of non-profit, with-profit and unit-linked policies. These are various ways you share in the investment gains of the insurance company you have chosen. So far we have looked at the broadly different structures of insurance policies. But within such a broad classification there are a great many varieties, particularly the way investments are made and how, as an investor, you are allowed to share in the returns.

Non-profit policy

Non-profit is a type of whole life or endowment policy. These are policies where a certain sum of money is guaranteed to you. If it is a whole life policy it becomes payable on your death, if it is endowment at the end of a specified period. A guaranteed sum sounds nice but there is a price you have to pay for it. The insurance company is reasonably conservative in assessing how this sum is arrived at and generally returns on non-profit policies are not very good.

These policies were very popular when people wanted to use them to pay off mortgages. Now that other types of policies can be used, non-profit policies have become less popular. But as a consumer there is one point you should bear in mind – the position of non-profit policies in the overall strategy of life companies. For a life company the profit they make on non-profit policies is very useful. Some companies have, in the past, used it to increase the bonus on with-profit policies and make it look attractive.

With-profit policy

In these policies you are sharing in the investment fortunes of the life companies. If the investment manager of the life company you have chosen does well, then so does your investment. You start off with a smaller sum insured compared to non-profits policies but to this is added the profits the insurance company makes while you have that policy. There is no way of knowing what your final pay-out will be. Every year the insurance company will announce a bonus based on how well the company's investments have done and on calculations worked out by the company's **actuary**. These are known as **reversionary bonuses**. There is no guarantee there will be a bonus every year but once the company has declared them they will be added to the sum assured and cannot normally be taken away. You should also benefit from what is called **terminal bonus**. This is your share of the surplus that may be in the pot as your policy comes to an end. So if your insurance company's investments do well over the life of your policy you will have higher reversionary and terminal bonuses and this will increase the money you get.

However, this system has its drawbacks. For a start the terms used are so incomprehensible that few people understand them. We need to understand what happens when the insurance company declares a reversionary or a terminal bonus. Every year the insurance company values its fund as it is required to do under the law. This seems simple enough but in practice it is quite complicated. Let us assume that the insurance company's investments have done very well and it could declare a large bonus. However, a bonus once declared cannot be taken away and, if, in future years the investments do not do quite as well, future bonuses will have to be lower – which could result in the sort of publicity insurance companies do not like. What happens in such a case is that an insurance company actuary, who is a cautious person at the best of times, works out a modest reversionary bonus. This does not so much reflect how well the company's investments have done that year but is more of an *indication* of the way in which the actuary is thinking about the likely future trends.

The actuary compensates for this when he comes to making

the calculations for **terminal bonus** – the final pay-out. Terminal bonuses are only paid on policies maturing during that year. So if you have a high value one year there is no guarantee that it would have to continue at that level next year when investment returns may not be that good. Terminal bonuses do increase the value of the policy. But in bad times there may be no terminal bonus. During the stockmarket crash of 1974/75 many companies cut their terminal bonuses. We have seen something similar following the October 1987 crash. So what you can get is an unofficial subsidy system. One group of policyholders may subsidise another group depending on the state of the investment market. Policyholders do not understand the system and many professionals see it as a clumsy one.

An alternative is unit-linked insurance and, indeed, it was the threat of this that forced many life companies to start providing terminal bonuses with-profit policies.

How do you compare bonuses?

This is another difficult area. Is, for instance, a simple bonus of 5% better than a compound bonus of 4% ? That will depend on the starting point. The life company which seems to give a lower bonus may have a higher initial sum assured so the return your money is getting is better. The best way to compare is to assume you are prepared to pay £10 a month and see what bonuses are payable at the end of 10, 20 and 30 years. Magazines such as *Money Management* and *Planned Savings* regularly publish statistics which provide some guidance. Even so, nobody can guarantee the returns in the future and this should be borne in mind when you choose your life company.

Low cost, with-profit policies

You can have a policy which combines low cost and with profits endowment policies. On death a high sum is assured through a non-profit policy or a low assured sum supplemented with bonuses if this produces a bigger figure. However, if you survive the term of the policy you receive a sum calculated on a with-profit basis. This policy is used a great deal to provide cover for an **endowment mortgage policy**.

Unit-linked life insurance

Whereas you do not know how your with-profits investments have done except when bonus declarations are made, in unit-linked policies the investments are expressed in **units**. The value of the units is determined by the value of the underlying investments. These may be units of an authorised unit trust which is either operated by an insurance company or by a **unit trust management group.** Many insurance companies create **special units** within their insurance fund. Your money would be invested in a variety of funds: equities, property, fixed-interest, or a mixture of these often called managed funds, or even just left on deposit. The prices of the units are quoted in the newspapers so you can easily see how your investment is doing.

But (similar to with-profit policies) such disclosure means that with a unit-linked policy you cannot be sure how much money you will get when the policy matures. That will depend on the final value of your units and should the policy mature just when investment times are bad you could find yourself badly done by. In general, unit-linked plans are of no advantage if you want your money back at specific times. Also, if you need to make payments at a certain time, say for **school fees**, or to meet the cost of sending your child to **university**, and you are relying on the policy you may discover that the units are doing badly at that particular moment and the policy does not provide you with enough money. Neither, of course, will a traditional with-profits policy. If a unit-linked contract is used for repaying a mortgage then some insurers provide regular policy reviews to ensure that the policy will enable you to meet the mortgage repayment.

If you are going to have a whole life policy then it mght be more useful to look at whole life unit-linked rather than endowment. With endowment if you have to withdraw money before it reaches maturity you will receive a poor return on your investment. With unit-linked whole life you should be able to cash in the full value of your units after a given time, and you can go on paying premiums up to an age that suits you.

Based on the broad principles we have described, life companies are continually coming up with new products that combine life insurance and investment. Some of these investment plans have had to be revised after the withdrawal of tax relief on life assurance premiums. These range from almost pure investment plans to those that combine investment with protection.

Also in the investment category come the single premium bonds where you pay a lump sum which the insurance company after deducting charges, etc, invests in units. Such bonds can also be combined with a cash plan in which you withdraw a certain sum of money each year.

Annuities

You can also use an insurance company to buy an annuity where you either pay a lump sum or a series of annual premiums and the insurance company repays this sum plus the investment income it has earned on it in the form of a **guaranteed income**. Annuities are used extensively when a person retires. For a man of 65 the average expectation of life is just over fourteen and a half years. So half the men in that age group will live beyond 80, the other half will not. In providing an annuity the insurance company is assessing the risk of the man living beyond 80 and if the man who has taken out the annuity does so then he can gain substantially. There are various kinds of annuities depending on when the person wants the income to start. However, on the whole annuities are for people who are well into retirement, men in their seventies, and women over 75 who are willing to sacrifice capital for income. A couple could have a **joint annuity** but here you need to keep a careful watch that it does not reduce after the first death.

The problem with annuities is that the original investment is not returned on death. You can get a **capital protected annuity** but this will generally produce a lower income and is not always easy to arrange, particularly if the person is old. You can use annuities to meet inheritance tax problems or to meet school fees but they remain rather a specialised investment. Income from annuity depends on interest rates – the higher the rates the higher the income from annuity. It also depends on the policy of the company. Does it want to expand its business in this area? If so it might offer a very keen annuity rate.

What happens when you become ill?

Nobody likes being sick but at some stage or the other it happens to all of us. The problem arises when you have to cope with serious illness, injury or disability which prevents you from earning your main income – or at least a substantial part of it – for some considerable length of time. The State can be of some help in this case and if you are an employee of a firm, your employer may make some provision. But the State provision is of the minimum kind and employers' sickness provisions vary considerably. If you are in full-time employment you should check what sort of sickness provisions your employer has. It is possible that your company is part of a health plan whereby your salary, or a substantial part of it, will be paid to you even while you are sick.

As an employee you receive **Statutory Sick Pay (SSP)** from your employer for the first 28 weeks of disability in any one tax year. The level of benefit is fixed according to your average earnings before disability. From April 1988 these rates were £49.20 if your average weekly earnings were £79.50 or more a week, or £34.25 if your average earnings were £41 to £79.49 a week. You do not get SSP if your average earnings were less than £41 a week. You cannot get extra SSP for children or other dependants. This figure changes every year and average earnings is, in broad terms, the last eight weeks earnings ending with the last pay date before you become ill. If you are not entitled to SSP or are self-employed, then provided you have satisfied certain minimum contribution requirements you can claim State sickness benefits. You can also get short term state sickness benefit for the first 28 weeks of a period of disability excluding any period for which SSP is payable. The amount you will receive will vary – check with your local DHSS office to ascertain the correct amount.

Invalidity Benefit starts after 28 weeks and consists of:

Invalidity Pension

This is £41.15 per week for a single person, £24.75 for an adult dependant and £8.40 of each dependant child (1988 rates).

Additional Invalidity Pension

This is not available to the self-employed. It is quite a complex calculation which is worked out as a percentage of the upper and lower earnings limit. Each year's benefits are subsequently increased in line with the national average earnings and ultimately the additional pension will be calculated by reference to the best 20 years over a person's record.

Invalidity Allowance

This amounts to £8.65 per week if disability commences before age 40, £5.50 if it commences between 40 and 50 and £2.75 if disability commences after 50 but before 55 for women or 60 for men.

But as you can see all this is unlikely to provide a replacement for the income you had or even meet the medical expenses you incur. These might involve private treatment, extra costs of transport, etc, if you are ill in hospital, or nursing and domestic attention if you are being looked after at home. If you are self-employed the position might be much worse since serious illness or disability may mean that you suddenly lose all, or nearly all of your income, and there is no company scheme to fall back on.

What is the answer?

Clearly, some form of insurance is essential. You can either have **sickness and accident policies** or **permanent health insurance**. Sickness and accident policies are basically short term. They run for a maximum of a year or two but they are popular because in some policies you can get a weekly payment or even a lump sum within seven days of temporary, total or partial disability. You can have policies where accidents and sickness are specified or policies which cover all accidents and all sicknesses. But the major disadvantage is that when the annual renewal time for such policies arrives the insurer can refuse renewal if there is a deterioration in the policyholder's health or other circumstances affecting the risk.

Your ability to get such insurance and how much you have to pay for it will depend on:

- Your health
- Your age
- Your occupation. Insurance companies classify occupation according to classes and different premiums are charged.

This type of insurance also specifies, in fairly strict terms, when you will be paid. Some insurance policies are restrictively worded and specify that you have to be permanently disabled from gainful employment of any and every kind before you can expect payment. Others may say that you have to be permanently disabled from your usual occupation or any other occupation for which you were fitted by knowledge and training. The most flexible policy wording is one which allows for permanent disablement from the insured person's usual occupation, although this may cost more.

You cannot use such policies to earn more than your normal pay when you are ill. For example, say your normal weekly pay is £400, but you insure yourself for a number of policies so that if you fall sick you could earn £600. Insurance companies try and prevent this by asking whether you have any other personal accident or sickness policies as they feel that otherwise you would be tempted to 'remain sick' and not go back to work. You can get round this by buying policies which pay lump sums but then you would pay very high premiums and not gain much overall. Such policies also specify conditions which if present would make the policy invalid. These can include deliberately injuring yourself, or becoming mad – though madness is not defined – or taking drugs, becoming an alcoholic, or exposing yourself to needless peril, eg, visiting a dangerous area such as Beirut, or trying to commit suicide. Some of these exclusions can be removed by paying a higher premium but most cannot.

What you need to know about taking out such policies is when do they start paying out. Generally, there is what is called a **deferment period**. In other words, you have to wait a few days after disablement for the policy to pay. A deferment period can be a few days or a few weeks depending on the policy. A somewhat similar process is achieved through franchise where, unless you are off work for a certain number of days, say seven, the policy will not start paying. There can be longer deferment periods and, in general, the longer the deferment the lower the premium. Such policies may also state that they will not start for sometime after you have taken out the policy. This could vary from a few weeks to a couple of years depending on the policy.

Permanent health insurance

This is increasingly becoming a popular form of health insurance. As with so much of insurance the name does not quite convey what this insurance does. For here, the permanent part refers to the insurance not the health. Very simply, it provides you income in case of long term disability or illness.

PHI, as it is popularly known, has been a part of many employers' contracts for a long time. But individuals have been slow to recognise how useful this policy can be. This is partly because insurance companies have not, until recently, been very good at marketing such policies. Often, they have been treated as loss-leaders. Also, some companies have used them as marketing tools to break into the pensions market. The policies are difficult to underwrite. But now there is growing realisation from companies that such policies can be useful earners and there is likely to be greater marketing stress on such policies. Much of this marketing drive is aimed at the self-employed. Permanent health insurance is also marketed under the title of **Income Protection Plan** – the impetus for such plans comes from the fact that a person is more likely to suffer continuous disablement for at least five months than to die before the age of 65.

A PHI policy will pay you an income while you are disabled following an accident or illness. This income can continue till you reach retirement age. You can pay premiums monthly or annually but, generally, monthly premiums cost a little more than annual premiums. Some policies have a **waiver of premium** clause which means that while you are being paid on a claim, you do not have to pay premiums. You may have to pay extra for this option. In some policies the final year or years of insurance may be premium-free.

A PHI policy is one of those policies which you never want to claim so you want to have the best cover whilst paying the least premium. This is determined by two considerations: when you want the policy to start paying and the type of job you are in.

Deferment period

This defines the period after which the policy will start paying you an income. You can decide that you would like your PHI policy to start paying you an income four weeks after your disablement, or it could be 13 weeks, 26 weeks or even a year or longer. The deferment period you choose will depend on your income and what other sources of funds you have to keep you going before the PHI policy pays. If your employer provides sick pay then you can defer receiving PHI until such time as the employer's sick pay ceases. Indeed, many policies will not start paying PHI until the employer's sick pay has stopped. If you are self-employed then you must judge how much of your own funds you can use to tide over your position before claiming PHI.

This may seem like an odd idea. After all, an insurance policy is meant to protect. So if you are disabled and cannot work and earn your income, the sooner the policy pays, the better. The problem is, the longer the period of deferment the lower the premium and since this is a policy you never hope to collect you are aiming to keep your premiums low.

Occupation

This is the all important thing in PHI. It will determine whether or not you are eligible for PHI. Insurance companies are very strict about who they are willing to give PHI contracts to and at what rates. If you are in the 'wrong' profession you could find yourself paying out a lot of money or not being able to secure PHI cover at all.

Here is a selection of how Permanent Health Insurance classify various professions – 1 being the standard rate, 2 is standard rate plus 10% , 3 is standard rate plus 30%, 4 standard rate plus 40%, RC means refer to company, NQ is no quote and SOC is a special occupation clause added to policy in view of the nature of duties or standard of fitness required.

1	– Accountant (other than Turf accountant)
RC	– Actor/Actress
3	– Baker
NQ	– Barmaid, Barman
NQ	– Bookmaker, Turf accountant
2	– Car salesman
NQ	– Chimney Sweep
RC	– Entertainer
2	– Dog Breeder
NQ	– Gaming club manager and other staff
2+SOC	– Police
3	– Milkman
3	– Traffic Warden
NQ	– Window cleaner

Of course, different companies classify occupations in different ways. One company's no quote occupation may well be standard rate plus 30% with another company. So it is worth shopping around. Obviously, the lower your classification, the lower your premium. Being a woman is a distinct disadvantage when it comes to arranging PHI. Many companies refuse to cover housewifes and other women often find that their premiums are as much as 50% cent more than their male counterparts. A male bricklayer would have difficulty in obtaining PHI cover, a female bricklayer might find it impossible.

What can you hope to receive?

Generally, the maximum you can expect to receive is calculated by taking three-quarters of your normal income and deducting National Insurance benefits (excluding those payable for dependants) and any other benefits payable as a result of your disability from whatever source. Some companies set lower limits, two-thirds for earnings above a certain amount. For very high earnings, the limit may be 55% of earnings above a specified level. You can protect what you get either through an **index-linked policy** or through one which provides automatic increases in benefits. Any payment you receive is **subject to income tax** but the Inland Revenue will not tax you until you have received payment for at least one complete tax year.

What happens when you return to work?

PHI payment will cease once you are back to your job full-time. If you can only return to the job on a part-time basis or have to take up a less demanding and hence less lucrative job, then the policy will pay an amount to make up the income you are losing. This is generally known as **rehabilitation benefit**, and starts only after 13 weeks of total incapacity and when a full claim has been admitted. Such payments normally stop after 52 weeks or on the person reaching the age of 60, whichever is earlier.

If, however, as a result of your disability you obtain a permanent part-time or lower paid job different to the one you had before then you can receive partial payments until retirement age. You cannot, of course, get any PHI payment once you reach the age of 65 for a man or the age of 60 for a woman. But the advantage of PHI is that once the policy has been issued, the insurers cannot refuse to renew the policy even if your health has become poor and you have claimed. Moreover, premiums cannot be increased on these grounds.

What happens when you retire?

You could rely on the State. Provided you have contributed sufficient years to the National Insurance fund you will be entitled to the basic State pension. But this can hardly be enough. Such a philosophy prompted the 1978 Social Security Reform which introduced the **State Earnings Related Pension Scheme, SERPS**, which is intended to supplement the basic state pension by providing an earnings-related pension within certain earnings limit. However, with the current Government's drive for privatisation, SERPS has come under attack and it is an open question as to how effective it will be after the year 2000 in providing people with a living wage when they retire.

This probably does not concern those employed in firms with good pension schemes. Their basic state pension could always be supplemented by that provided by an employer. But few people these days work all their life for one employer. We are all likely to work for several employers during our lifetime and every time you change jobs you reduce the amount of the final pension you can get.

The solution to these problems is provided in recent legislative changes which allows nearly everybody to get a **personal pension**. You can either opt out of your employer's scheme or opt out of the State Earnings Related Pension Scheme by setting up your own personal pension. If you are under 45 it could make sense to opt out of SERPS, but if your company pension scheme is a good one, you should stay in it – regardless of age.

Why a pension plan?

After your own home a pension plan is one of the best investments you can have and has excellent tax advantages. It can be looked upon as an insurance against not being able to earn an income due to age, rather than illness. Any contributions you make up to a certain limit are tax-free. The money in the fund grows in a tax-free environment. At the end of the day you can take up to 25% of the fund being used to provide you with a pension, under the newly introduced personal pensions, as a tax-free lump sum. On top of that you will get a regular income. It is important to realise the difference between personal pensions and the pension scheme that your employer may run.

In personal pensions the limit of how much you can invest is defined as 17½% of net relevant earnings; this increases as you grow older and reaches 27½% for those aged between 61–75. There is no limit on the amount of pension you can have. In a company scheme you cannot have a pension which is more than two-thirds of your final salary. If you are in SERPS then the government is giving an inducement to encourage you to withdraw and set up your own personal pension plan, funded by part of your NI contributions.

A pension is a **deferred annuity**. Over a period of time you pay money into a fund, be it that of your company or your own. This is generally managed by a financial organisation. When you retire you use the money collected to buy an annuity which gives you a regular income. In a pension plan it is not necessary to go to the financial organisation in which you invested your money to obtain this annuity. You can shop around to see which insurance companies provide the best rate and exercise what is known as the **open market option**.

Small self-administered schemes

There are various kinds of pension plans but one that is worth looking at in some detail is the small self-administered scheme (SSAS). These sort of schemes are very useful for partnerships and small companies since the partners or directors have a great deal of control and say in where the money they are investing in their pension fund goes. Also, if properly advised they can use such schemes to provide themselves with very useful tax planning.

Take an example of a successful family business owned jointly by husband and wife. Taxable profits of £160,000 are forecast for the current year after directors' total remuneration. The company wishes to purchase new office/warehouse premises of £400,000. It decided to set up an SSAS with a first year contribution of £100,000. The trustees of the scheme will then borrow £300,000 and purchase the property in the Fund.

Points to watch

The Inland Revenue will be concerned if it is obvious that the small self-administered scheme has been set up merely to buy property. It might be advisable to do the property purchase in the second year of the scheme and there should be an intention to pay future pension contributions to the scheme. Also, the revenue will usually regard borrowings in excess of three times the normal annual contribution as an indication that the bonafides are questionable.

If the major or sole asset of the fund is a property the members should normally be at least ten years from retirement date to ensure sufficient liquidity at that time to pay benefits.

A qualified surveyor will be required to confirm the value of the property including the rental value and a commercial lease will be drawn up for the occupation of the premises.

Benefits will be based on final salary which is defined for a controlling director as 'the average of the total emoluments for any period of three or more consecutive years ending not earlier than 10 years before normal retirement date'. It is, therefore, important to establish at least three high earning years in the past 12, to ensure that a maximum tax-free lump sum and pension can be provided.

There is a potential problem; that of an **unexpected death** requiring a realisation of the fund's assets in the early years of the scheme and just after the parents' retirement. During these years it may be advisable to buy **term assurance** policies on members lives to protect this risk. Property often forms the best introduction to small self-administered schemes but soon most people realise the long term benefits of such schemes.

7 Insurance for the small businessman

If you are in business on your own or with partners then you need to look at insurance very carefully. Your business may involve working from home or having an office. But whatever the position, insurance cover is vital to protect you and your business should things go wrong.

Let us take the simplest case. You have a part-time business you run from home which involves a secretary coming to your home once or twice a week to sort out your correspondence and other administrative work. Now you may not think of insurance cover in this case but what happens if she should trip over a wire and injure herself? She could **sue you for damages**. Would you be covered in such a case? It is possible that your ordinary household insurance will cover you for this but if you are using your house as a workplace it may not.

Employer's liability insurance

If you have a proper office, separate from home, and you employ people, the law requires you to have insurance to cover employers' liability. All employers must insure against their legal liability for **injury** to employees or **disease** sustained by them arising from their employment. If you employ close relatives you may not require this insurance but you need to check that. You must insure for at least £2 million but in practice most policies offer unlimited liability.

The law also requires you to exhibit a certificate of employers' liability at each place of work.

Other liability insurance

In addition you would be well advised to insure for **public liability** and **product liability**. Public liability covers legal liability to pay damages to members of the public for death or injury or for damage to their property which occurs as a result of your business activities. Such insurance will also cover legal fees, costs and expenses incurred because of the accident.

You have to be careful in choosing the amount of the insurance known as the **limit of indemnity**. The trend has been for higher amounts to be awarded for personal injury and property damage so make sure the figure you have settled on is a realistic one. The limit of indemnity relates to claims arising from a single incident.

If you make, repair or sell objects you could be held legally liable for damage or injury arising from them and you should take out a product liability insurance. It generally covers you for a maximum amount each year.

Motor insurance

If your business has cars then the law requires that you insure the cars for the requirements of the Road Traffic Acts. In practice you would obtain **comprehensive insurance** policies which are very similar to the type of cover individuals can get for their cars. Insurance companies will need complete details of the type of cars you have, the use made of them and, if you carry passengers, the maximum number of such fare-paying passengers. You can get a no-claims bonus on car insurance but at a lower rate than that for individuals. If you have a fleet of cars then what is known as a fleet policy can be arranged and the premiums you will pay will depend on the claims record of the fleet. There is a limit of around £1 million on third party property damage.

Property

Broadly speaking, the insurance is similar to the type you would have for your home but there are obviously special factors. You should insure the buildings and the contents of your business against fire and additional perils such as explosion, riot, malicious damage, storm, flood, impact by aircraft, escape of water from tanks or pipes and sprinkler leakage. In the case of contents insurance you should insure your stock for its cost price. You can make some provision for seasonal stock fluctuation and if you have proper protection theft cover is not difficult to arrange. But loss of stock by **pilferage is excluded**. You should also have **goods in transit insurance** to cover against loss or damage whilst goods are being sent by carriers or in your vehicles. Normally, the sum insured is either a limit on each consignment or for each vehicle.

The law requires that some items of plant and machinery be inspected regularly and this can be part of an insurance policy. It is common to have a policy that provides for replacement as new cover but if you choose indemnity then you will find that wear and tear of the plant and machinery in the course of your business will be taken into account when claims are settled.

It is common to have **all risks** cover for money and this would extend to cash, cheques, notes and postage stamps. The amount for which you will be covered will depend on whether the insurance is for business hours or outside it and the location of the money: at your place of business, in a safe, at your home, or that of one of your directors or employees or in transit. The insurance company may ask for safes to be installed and certain precautions taken when money is in transit.

Business interruption

This policy will provide for the shortfall in profits together with any increased cost of working and extra accountants fees in providing verification of amounts claimed should your business be interrupted by some disastrous event. When you take out such a cover you will need to estimate the maximum time needed to start your business working normally and the sum insured must cover this period of time. The insurance company will want to know your anticipated gross profit; if later the audited figure turns out to be lower you may get a refund of premiums.

As a small businessman there are certain other insurances you should consider:

- **Fidelity** to protect you against loss should one of your employees turn out to be dishonest
- **Frozen food.** If your business involves having frozen food in deep freezers on your premises then you should cover them against breakdown or damage or failure of electricity supply
- If your business involves running a shop then insurance to provide for **replacement of plate glass** following malicious or accidental damage is necessary
- It is a sound idea to get **legal expenses insurance** to cover legal fees should your business become involved in litigation
- You can also obtain cover for yourself and your employees for **personal injury** sustained during theft or attempted theft

- If your business involves travelling then **travel insurance** covering the range we have discussed should be taken out.

Insurance for yourself and your partners or directors

The most important part of a small business is the small businessman himself – you. You need insurance cover to protect yourself and your partners so that if something happens your business does not suffer unduly.

If you are on business on your own then you are responsible for all loans or credit facilities you use in the course of business. Sickness or incapacity could jeopardise these loans and mean serious disruption to your business. If you die your business could experience transitional problems as it passes to a family member or ceases to trade.

You can secure the loans and credit facilities you enjoy by an appropriate **term assurance** for the period of the loan. If the loan is to be repaid on a capital and interest basis at regular intervals then **a decreasing term assurance**, like the sort of policy that covers mortgage repayments, may be most suitable. If interest only is being repaid with capital being repaid at the end of the loan, **level term cover** may be more useful. An option to renew the loan should be considered if the period of the loan can be extended. The advantage of building in such an option in the policy is that it can be exercised without further evidence of health.

If, as a businessman on your own, you make use of a continuing credit facility which varies as your needs change then a level term assurance policy may also be useful. The best way of going about it is to select a sum assured based on the average size of loan. Renewal options can be considered if necessary.

As we have seen, to protect you against sickness or long term ill health it is very advisable that you should look at **Permanent Health Insurance**. To protect against death and the disruption that this would cause it is worth looking at with-profits whole life, low-cost whole life or a **unit-linked flexible whole life policy**. Such policies would protect you for the whole of your life and any problems of future insurability or higher premiums due to subsequent ill-health can be avoided.

It would probably be a wise idea to write the policy under trust for the benefit of those who would face problems in the event of untimely death. If this is done then those who are due to receive the benefit have a choice as to their use of proceeds. Money could be used for investment in the business either as an outright transfer or a loan for a period to be agreed. If the heirs do not want to continue the business the money could be used for non-business purposes such as providing your family with an alternative source of income.

You should be careful to make sure that the **taxation** aspects of any life insurance policy proceeds are looked at. If you have a qualifying policy, basically one that has been going for ten years, there are no liabilities to income tax or capital gains tax. However, in a **non-qualifying policy** you may be subject to higher income tax arising from any 'profit' on the policy if at the time of death or surrender of policy you are liable to higher rates of income tax. But since the 1988 Budget, with the higher rates having been lowered to 40%, this is not as severe as in the past.

It should be remembered that the *funds* in which your premiums are invested are subject to corporation tax and **capital gains tax**. The insurance company with which you take out a policy will meet these liabilities and then pay your proceeds but you cannot re-claim these taxes. Policies can be **written in trust** so that the policy proceeds do not form part of your estate for **inheritance tax purposes**. Payment of policy premiums are unlikely to attract inheritance tax liability as they would probably fall within what is your 'normal expenditure out of income exemption' or the annual allowance. As a small businessman on your own you should, of course, also look at suitable **retirement policies** as already discussed.

Key man insurance

You may be covered but what about some of the people you employ? One or more of them may be vital to your organisation. Without them your company may come to a grinding halt or be badly affected. You could lose profits, loan security or investment protection. Each business will have its own list of key personnel. It could be the research director whose ideas keeps the business going, or a Sales Manager whose skills in pushing up sales is exceptional. Generally, most companies would regard **directors** or **chief executives** as key men. If you are in business on your own then you probably occupy such a position yourself.

No two businesses are quite the same and the loss of profits that your business may suffer if you lose a key man will depend on whether it is a long term or a short term loss. In the short term it may affect your cash flow, or projects in which the key man was involved may be cancelled or you may have to incur additional expenses in recruiting and training someone to replace him. In the long term you may lose suppliers' goodwill and morale may be affected. The loss of a key man could also affect your company's ability to pay the interest on loans or even repay them.

If your company is newly formed then you may well find that those willing to invest will need insurance cover for key men. This may also apply if the company is embarking on a share flotation or issuing more shares. The key man in such cases could be an **important shareholder**.

For all these situations a suitable form of insurance would be a policy that gave life cover though in each case it may be a different kind of policy. For loss of profits a **level term assurance** policy may be best. You may have to say how long the employee is likely to remain in his key position and the policy could have an option so that should he or she continue for a longer period you could renew the policy without further evidence of health. It may also be useful to consider an option to increase the term assured. This does not have to match the growth in the key man's value but it can provide some extra cover without the need for further evidence of health. This form of level term insurances may also be suitable to cover credit facilities which vary with our business requirements.

To cover key men who are vital to loan security, term assurance for a decreasing sum to match the repayment of the loan may be the most suitable. If there is more than one key man involved then it is useful to effect **single life policies** with the sum assured being the proportion of the loan corresponding to each key man's value.

Insurance cover for investment protection is of a short term nature and the best policy would be level term assurance for a specified period to cover the share flotation or issue of additional shares. Options to renew the policy without evidence of health and increase the sum assured during the programme should also be considered.

In all these cases **permanent health insurance** should also be considered for a key man. This would pay you a regular sum to compensate for the loss. If this is meant to cover loss of profits then the period of deferment should be made to coincide with the time when the first expected profits will suffer. Generally, such policies have a deferment period of three months but you can have it extended if you wish. Remember, the longer the deferment, the lower the premium, so care should be taken to estimate when the loss of the keyman will affect profits. Usually, such policies are taken out for a period of between five and 10 years.

How much should you insure for?

To answer this question you should consider a variety of factors:

- The profit and track record of the last five years and projections for the next five years,
- the cash position,
- the likely loss of profit should a key man die,
- the cost of recruiting or training a replacement,
- the time it would take for the replacement to be as profitable as the keyman and the loss of profits this would involve,
- the loans likely to be called in if the key man died,
- if the key man's loss would affect special projects.

Calculation

The actual calculation can be based on two factors:

Multiple of salary

The key man's total remuneration package is taken into account and the multiple could be upto ten times this figure. But this takes no account of the key man's contribution to turnover.

Proportion of salary bill

The formula used is:

$$\frac{\text{key man's salary}}{\text{total salary/wages bill}}$$

This does not take turnover into account. If the key man is a shareholder who draws a small salary and reinvests profits into the business the figure could be distorted. Additionally, if a large number of employees earn relatively low wages the sum assured may not be as satisfactory.

Multiple of profits

Here you either take five times net profit or twice gross profit, gross profit being cost of turnover less cost of sales. For companies that are rapidly expanding such portions may change to three times gross profit and seven times net profit. Net profit is what remains after administration expenses but before tax. The problem here is that for tax purposes a company may have a low net profit which could distort the situation.

Taxation of policies

The premiums you pay on the policies may or may not be allowed as a deduction against tax. This will depend on your local Inspector of Taxes. The general principles that matter here are:

- The **sole relationship** between yourself and the key man should be that of employer and employee
- The employee may also be a shareholder provided the shareholding is not significant. This is generally considered to be a holding of less than 5% of the issued shares. But whatever the holding, if the shareholder is a **member of the family** which owns the company, premiums are unlikely to be allowed against tax
- The insurance is intended to meet **loss of profits** resulting from the loss of services to the employer
- and it is of a one year or **short term assurance**. The Inland Revenue regards five years or under as short term.

In addition to this, the policy must be wholly and exclusively to protect against loss of profits if you want premiums to be allowed for tax purposes. Thus if you are taking a key man policy to cover loan protection this may not be allowed for tax. It is important to realise that if a policy serves two objects, one of which is not allowed then all the premiums will not be deductible. Premiums cannot be apportioned.

Strictly speaking, only term assurance will meet the tax

criteria, other types of assurance being partly investment contract as they may have a surrender value. If premiums are allowed as a tax deduction, then proceeds from the policy will be taxed as trading receipt. If premiums have not been allowed then proceeds are regarded by the Revenue as of a capital nature and will generally not be taxed.

As regards the premiums on permanent health insurance these are allowable as a **business expense** provided the cover is annual or short term and the proceeds are payable to the employer to cover loss of profits. But since the premiums are paid in instalments the proceeds of the policy will be taxed as income. You should always clarify your tax position with your local Inspector of Taxes before deciding on the policies.

What happens if the key man leaves?

- You can make the policy paid-up so that you do not have to pay premiums and with a reduced amount payable on death. But this does mean keeping in touch with the key man which could be a problem
- You can surrender the policy
- You can continue paying premiums, but since this would mean keeping in contact with the key man this may be impractical
- You can assign the policy to the key man for his own use. You should be careful of how this is carried out as it could have important tax consequences or be done as part of a retirement policy.

Partnership insurance

In this country the **Partnership Act 1890**, supplemented by common and case law form the legal framework regulating partners affairs. Partnerships may vary in size from the husband and wife firm that runs the local electrical shop to some of our largest accountancy firms with hundreds of partners and thousands of staff members. But whatever the size the basic elements of partnership insurance remain the same. There are three fundamental considerations:

- Is the partnership covered so that the remaining partners can buy the share of the firm owned by the deceased partner?
- Do the partners who are continuing have the cash to buy out a retiring partner?
- Do they have the cash to help a partner retire?

A partnership agreement may say that if a partner dies the remaining partners can buy his share but if the cash is not available then this is not of much use. In such cases insurance policies can be useful. There are several options available.

1 Each of the partners takes out a **term insurance** policy on his **own life** which will benefit other partners if he should die. If he leaves the firm, other than through death, then the policy benefits his wife. If all the partners are of the same age then each pays his own premiums. If there are large age differences then the premiums should be pooled and the younger ones pay more than the older ones because they are likely to live longer and benefit more.
2 If you are in a partnership with two or three people then the **'other partner' trust method** might work quite well. What happens here is that you take out a term insurance policy on your own life on trust for the other partner. The sum insured is the amount the partner who is supposed to receive the money would need to buy your share. If there are three of you then each of you affect either one policy with the proceeds to be shared between the other two in some proportions already agreed, or two policies each in the required proportions.
3 If premiums are similar no problem arises. However, if you have partners with different ages then this will produce a sum insured on the older partner's life less than the amount the beneficiary partner needs to buy the older man's share. The solution would be a **'life of another'**

policy to provide the cover. In this method each partner calculates the amount he will need to buy his proportion of the share of a colleague and takes out a term insurance for this amount on life of another basis. His colleagues repeat this process.

What happens if you want to buy out a retiring partner?

The best way to go about this would be for the younger man to take out a policy that would be geared to the older man's retirement date. If there is a fixed retirement date then a with-profit **endowment policy** or fixed date **unit-linked policy** may suffice, but if the date is not certain then an open-ended unit-linked policy may be more suitable as this can allow the policy to be encashed at any time.

How much should you insure?

The sum should cover three considerations: the capital value of the partner's share in the business including partnership property; the forecast value of any undistributed profits at the date of death or retirement; the value of goodwill if this is included in a partnership account.

To take an example, let us assume that you are in partnership with two others. The senior partner has an interest in the partnership of £85,000, another one for £50,000 and you have a £40,000 interest. Each of you take out level term assurance to protect the partnership for the value of your capital until retirement age of let us say, 62. The senior partner who is 52 will pay an annual premium of £570 for the next ten years on his capital sum of £85,000. The other partner who is 43 will pay £210 for 19 years on £50,000. You, 37 years old, will pay £90 for the next 25 years.

If you decide to purchase your partners' interest in relation to existing interests then your senior partner's premium should be split in the ratio 50:40 between the two of you. Your 43 year old colleague's premium should be split 85:40 between you and the senior partner and your premium should be split 85:50 between your two colleagues. This calculation should be contrasted with what is actually paid and whoever has paid too much should be reimbursed by those who have paid too little.

Shareholder share purchase

Partnerships are not the only way small firms operate. They may be private companies with shareholders, some or all of whom may act as directors. What happens when a shareholder dies or wants to retire? Several problems could arise. If a shareholder dies his share could pass to his beneficiaries who may not want to carry on with the business, or may not be suitable. The shareholding may pass to a number of people, fragmenting the close control nature of the company. A beneficiary may sell the share to a third party and this could jeopardise the control of the company; a shareholder may want to retire and obtain a capital sum for his shares.

All these possibilities can be covered by **life insurance** in a manner similar to partnership insurance. The shareholders could agree on a buy and sell arrangement with the continuing shareholders purchasing the 'outgoing' shareholders shares. Alternatively, you could have what is known as a **cross option** or **double option agreement**. This will often be better for inheritance tax reasons. The shareholders will agree that on the death or retirement of a shareholder the continuing shareholders have an option to purchase the outgoing shareholder's shares. The policies affected under these plans are very similar to the ones we discussed when considering partnership insurance.

8 Insurance for the holidaymaker

Holidays are for fun, relaxation, enjoyment. But what happens if things go wrong? Your luggage does not arrive, your money is stolen, you are injured or fall sick? You might injure someone, or damage their property and have to pay costs. You may not even manage to have a holiday because it has had to be cancelled or cut short due to accident or sickness. Fifty per cent of all holiday claims concern cancelled holidays. If you are going on a package tour then you have to pay a deposit when you book the holidays and the balance of the money some weeks before you begin the holiday. Tour operators will only refund part of this money if you cancel and may not refund anything at all if you cancel on the day the holiday is supposed to commence.

Insurance for holidays comes either as:

1 A package – which provides cover for many different contingencies with limits fixed as to how much you can claim. In some package policies you are offered very limited cover at fairly low cost but you can top-up by increasing the cover under one or more specific sections depending on your individual requirements.
2 A selective policy – where you choose the different sections you want. Thus you may want only medical expenses and loss of money covered. You may find that such selection actually means paying more premiums. In some cases a selective policy can mean paying as much as a package policy but you may find that a selective policy is more generous in meeting a claim. With holiday insurance it is not so much underinsurance as overinsurance you must guard against. The all risks section of your **household**

contents policy will cover your personal belongings and medical expenses may be covered under a **medical bills insurance** scheme. So make sure you are not insuring twice over when you take out holiday insurance. For if you claim you will not be paid twice over.

Holiday insurance provides cover for various eventualities.

Cancellation

Holidays may have to be cancelled for several reasons. Insurance companies will not pay out on a claim if you cancel because you have changed your mind or cannot afford to go. You must be *forced* to cancel your holiday for a necessary and unavoidable reason in order to claim money on this policy. Some of the reasons for valid cancellation are:

- **Accident or injury** to yourself, spouse or other relative, travelling companion or close business associate. Relatives could be children, parents and in-laws. Fiancees may or may not be included. Such policies do not normally define close business associates but you cannot cancel and hope to successfully claim just because you are suddenly too busy at work to have a holiday
- Being put in **quarantine**
- Failure of tour operator, but your ability to claim money may depend on whether the tour operator was a member of the **Association of British Travel Agents** (**ABTA**) or a licensed coach operator or transport line
- Called for **jury service** or as a **witness** in a court of law
- A **fire or burglary** at your own home but you must be able to show that because of it you have to be at home
- If you or your spouse become **pregnant** after the policy has been taken out. If you knew you were pregnant when the policy was taken out you may not be able to claim and some insurers may not pay out even if you became pregnant after you booked your holiday
- If you have been made **redundant**, although not all policies provide such a cover

- Cancellations arising from **strikes** or **adverse weather** affecting the aircraft or ship departure.

Under the cancellation clause you can generally expect to receive between £1,000 and £3,500.

Curtailment

If you have good reasons for cutting short your holiday, and these are broadly the same as cancellation, then you may be able to claim for travelling home early by **scheduled flights** rather than on the booked charter flights.

Delay

The Spanish air traffic controllers are on strike, as they tend to be whenever the summer rush to the Costa Brava begins, so what can you do? Look, perhaps, to the delay clause of the policy which will compensate you if your departure is delayed beyond a specified period as a direct result of strike, industrial action, adverse weather or mechanical breakdown of the aircraft or sea vessel. The Insurance Ombudsman in his 1982 report held that delay caused by an **airport strike** is *not* covered by a travel policy unless mentioned. So check what your policy says.

Policies generally cover both outward and return journeys but often the cover will not operate unless the delay is at least of 12 hours. Under some policies you may be able to claim anything between £50 and £300 if you miss your flight or boat because of failure of public transport. But this does not apply if you are travelling by private car. You can also obtain cover if you are prevented from reaching your destination because the aircraft has been **hijacked** and policies will reimburse reasonable expenses that you may incur as a result of hijacking. The amount you get under this section will depend on how long the delay is but this is usually limited to between £60 and £100 per person insured.

Personal accident

If, as a result of an accident you should die, lose a limb or an eye or suffer permanent total disablement there can be a claim under holiday insurance. In some policies loss of limb means actual physical severance of an arm or a leg although some others include loss of use of the limb. Loss of eye can mean actual physical loss of the eye itself and loss of sight. Permanent total disablement means that you are so severely injured that even 12 months after the accident you cannot return to work in any form. Some policies are less restrictive and allow you to claim if you cannot return to the type of work you are suited to by knowledge and training. For temporary total disablements you may be able to get weekly payments but these are not generally available under package policies. Also, when a weekly payment is made, students, housewives, pensioners or children may not qualify.

The amount of claim you can make ranges widely, with the lump sum varying from £4,500 up to £25,000 with restrictions on the amount that the young and the old (those over 70) can get.

Loss of baggage

Policies limit how much you can be compensated for loss of baggage or even the amount you can claim for a single item. The single item limit varies from £150 to £250. If you have individual items worth more than that it is advisable to consider covering it under the all risks extension to your household contents policy. Some policies pay on a replacement as new basis, some on an intrinsic value or indemnity basis. If luggage is lost in transit or delayed, your policy may pay for essentials you may need to buy, up to a certain amount – say £50 or £100.

Loss of money

Most policies will have a definition of money, and that could include passport, coupons, vouchers, tickets and green card. You are unlikely to be covered if you lose money because you had a bad exchange rate or were short changed by a local trader. There is a limit on the amount of money refunded, varying from £150 to £300.

Medical expenses

This is, probably, one of the main reasons why most people take out holiday insurance. Hospital treatment and medical expenses abroad can be very expensive particularly in the USA or Canada.

Insurance companies do not much care for what they call 'pre-existing' medical conditions, which may mean something you have suffered six months before the holiday or even before that. In one case, cover was meant to provide for 'serious injury or illness occurring after insurance has been affected' which resulted in 'necessary and unavoidable' cancellation. The chronically ill relative who was supposed to be covered took a serious turn for the worse and the policyholder claimed. She felt that while her relative was ill the deterioration was sudden and unexpected and that illustrated the type of situation the insurance company should protect. The insurance company disagreed and the policyholder complained to the Insurance Ombudsman. He concluded that, 'the illness occurred long before the policy was effected and the event, which had to do with its progress, was not covered under the policy'.

The Ombudsman's view is that since travel insurance is so cheap it can cope with a healthy man falling sick, but not for a sick person suffering a relapse. This could be a matter for debate but what is clear is that insurance policies regarding travel are not always clearly worded and they are presented in a fashion meant to confuse. The terms of the policy are often in small print and hidden away in a brochure which concentrates on the sun, the sand and the beaches the holiday offers. In such circumstances it is easy not to see that for the policy to be valid you need to produce a medical certificate. Most insurance companies have little to do with the layout of the brochure and matters are not helped by the fact that in the anticipation of the holiday people do not read their travel policies. Even when they do they do not always understand it. So a man who, against medical advice, brought his entire family back from the USA because of a mild case of gastroenteritis could not understand why his insurance company would not pay. It is imperative that you make a point of searching out and reading the policy document and ensuring that you have the insurance you need.

Policies cover medical treatment, hospital and nursing charges and any additional travel and/or accommodation expenses because of illness. If you are travelling in a group policies generally pay for the cost of travel and hotel expenses of one of your group who may need, on medical grounds, to stay with you or escort you home. But they will not pay for a relative to fly over and join you.

If you have to go into hospital policies usually pay a set sum per day in addition to hospital charges but are unlikely to pay a weekly disablement benefit. Policies will also pay to get you back home for treatment and in the case of death the cost of transporting the body or the ashes, or paying for the funeral arrangements abroad.

How much do you need to pay?

In the **EEC** and other countries you may be able to take advantage of the health or **welfare schemes** of that country. In order to do this, before you travel, you need to check details with the **DHSS** by getting the appropriate form which provides details about the medical treatment you can get for free in Europe and the paperwork you need to have with you to use the medical facilities in those countries. Generally, holiday policies require you to pay an excess which vary from section to section and can range from £5 to £20.

All policies carry standard exclusions, so you are not covered for war and kindred risks, ie, civil war, revolution, insurrection. If you cancel a holiday because you fear hostilities will be declared you are unlikely to be covered, although you may get a Lloyd's policy to cover you. You will need to check your policy carefully to find out what the exclusions are.

What you pay will depend on how long you want the policy for and where you are visiting. As a general rule, the further away you go from the UK the higher the premium. Normally, there are three basic territorial rating areas; UK, Europe and worldwide which normally attracts the highest premium. Different insurers may define these areas in an idiosyncratic fashion – all insurance companies have different ways of defining the finer points of the policies with the result that all sorts of categories are included in the various sections.

Premiums also depend on how long you have the policy in force. Policies generally cover a time span. So there may be one premium for a seven-day trip and if your journey lasts eight days you will fall into the next, higher, premium category. However, if you take out a twenty-day policy and return home on the fifteenth day that is when the policy ceases. The company will not meet any claims for what happens to you between days 16 and 20 even though you have paid the premium for those days. But, if in circumstances beyond your control your trip has been extended beyond the period of insurance, the cover can continue till you complete the journey, or for a set number of days. Such extensions vary from policy to policy and you need to check the wording of your policy carefully.

Who sells holiday insurance?

You can get holiday insurance direct from an insurance company, from the broker who arranges your house and other insurances or even your local bank manager. But more often than not if you are travelling on a package holiday, holiday insurance is either part of the package or an optional extra. Sometimes **tour operators** assume you would need holiday cover and include it unless you state otherwise, sometimes you are required to tick a box on the booking form saying yes or no to holiday cover.

If you are making your own arrangements then your **travel agent** should be able to arrange holiday insurance for you. Generally, you will find that the bigger travel agents have their own insurance arm to arrange for such insurance. If you have forgotten all about it and remember just as you get to the airport then you can buy insurance there from slot meters which provide personal accident or death compensation. There is usually no limit on the cover but you may find you are paying rather a lot for such policies.

Emergency assistance

It is now common for holiday insurance policies to include round the clock emergency assistance. This provides for the cost of medical treatment abroad, for the return home of the patient and the travel expenses of the remaining members of the party. Specially equipped ambulance-type aircraft may also be used to repatriate patients accompanied by doctors. Such medical emergency assistance is provided by **specialised companies** like Mondial and while you can get this insurance cover from them directly, most travel insurers link up with them to provide such cover as part of their package. It is a feature of such 24-hour emergency assistance service that you are a provided with a telephone number. It is often a telephone number in this country and you can reverse the charges if necessary. So before you leave home make sure you have the number. The range of such service varies but they operate in the main commercial and holiday centres of the world.

Special travel schemes

As we have seen, if you are beyond a certain age limit, or too infirm, the standard cover may not be extended to you. To cater for this category special travel schemes have been developed, such as **senior citizens clubs** and associations for the **disabled** where insurers have arrived at appropriate premiums and terms based on the sort of claims they have had in the past. Insurance tailored for the **business traveller** is also available which in some ways is ironic since travel insurance began with business executives making overseas visits. Specialised cover for drivers of road haulage vehicles (as they travel all over Europe) is also available.

Group travel arrangements

Insurers also have schemes especially tailored for employers whose employees make a number of business trips outside the UK. Such policies cover medical and other expenses, cancellation charges, loss of baggage and money and personal accident. Policies can also be extended to cover families of employees travelling abroad. The exclusion clauses vary between insurers and in such policies providing for pregnancy, or for people over 75 can be subject to negotiation.

9 Insurance for the car owner and driver

The law requires that you cannot drive a motor car without insurance. But the legal requirement is the absolute minimum. All you have to insure for are injuries sustained by other people, including passengers, during a road accident with another vehicle. This is known as act-only policy and insurers do not encourage these. Most people take out insurance which provides a much greater range of cover. Two out of three motorists hold **comprehensive policies** and the remainder **third party, fire and theft** or **third party** only. You can take out an insurance policy to cover: third party only which will cover liability for injuries caused to other people and to passengers in the car, liability of passengers in the car for accidents caused by them, as well as liability for damage to other people's property; third party, fire and theft; or comprehensive insurance.

The cover provided by these policies is summarised in the chart on pages 94–95.

Driving other people's cars

If you drive someone else's car you will usually be covered under your own policy provided you are driving with the owner's permission. But it is always worthwhile to check that this is so. The cover, however, is limited to the liabilities insured under a third party policy so that any damage you do to the car borrowed will not be covered under your own policy. On a borrowed car you do *not* get the same cover as

Insurance cover available

1 Liability for injuries to other people, arising from accidents caused by your car on public roads or elsewhere. Legal costs incurred with your insurance company's consent in connection with a claim against you will also be paid.

2 Liability for injuries to passengers in your car.

3 Liability of passengers in your car in respect of accidents caused by them – for example, the careless opening of a door causing injury to a passer-by or damage to his property.

4 Liability for damage to other people's property. For example, if you are involved in an accident which causes damage to another car, your insurance company will pay all or part of the cost of repairs to the other car, depending on the extent to which you are legally to blame.

5 Liability for injuries to other people or damage to their property caused by a trailer or caravan attached to your car.

6 Fire or theft – but if your car is not normally kept in a locked garage at night your insurer may exclude theft, make theft cover subject to special conditions or charge an extra premium.

THIRD PARTY FIRE AND THEFT Sections 1 to 6

THIRD PARTY Sections 1 to 5

7 Accidental damage to your car but not wear and tear, depreciation, loss of use, mechanical or electrical breakdown and punctures. If, at the time of the accident, your car is being driven by or is in the charge of someone who holds a provisional licence or has held a full licence for less than a year, or who is under 25 years old, you will usually have to pay for damage to your car up to a maximum stated in your policy. This 'excess' will generally be from £25 onwards.

8 Accidents to yourself and perhaps your wife or husband, resulting in death or loss of sight and/or limbs, up to stated amounts. This applies to all journeys in your private car or in any other car not belonging to you whether you are driving or not. This benefit applies only to policies in the name of an individual.

9 Medical expenses up to a stated amount incurred by you or your passengers as a result of an accident involving your car.

10 Loss of, or damage to rugs, clothing and personal effects up to a stated amount while they are in the car.

COMPREHENSIVE
Sections 1 to 10.

ACT ONLY
This type of cover is restricted to liability for injuries to other people, including your passengers, in traffic accidents on public roads. Act only policies are limited to the minimum compulsory requirements of the Road Traffic Act 1972.

Source: Association of British Insurers

you get driving your own car on a comprehensive policy. So if you are borrowing someone else's car make sure he or she has a comprehensive policy on an any-driver basis. If you are covered by a comprehensive policy as a spouse on a **'named driver and spouse only'** basis that insurance does not cover you while driving anybody else's vehicle. In such a situation, if the car you have borrowed is uninsured then the spouse would be committing an illegal act by driving the car.

The Insurance Ombudsman has pointed out that in these days when so many families run two cars it is unwise to insure each car for 'owner only' driving. If it becomes necessary for a spouse to drive the other's car, cover may be reduced to the basic requirements of the Road Traffic Acts. The recommendation is that cover under each policy should be extended to at least both owners and preferably to all drivers with permission. Even so, it is worth remembering that no policy will cover accidental damage to any other car. Borrowed cars are only covered under their own insurance policies, if at all.

Insurers will not look kindly on those who have a son or daughter's car insured 'in the parents name' in order to save on premium. The Insurance Ombudsman has held that this is nothing less than outright cheating and that not only can the insurer cancel the policy, he can also deduct a suitable charge from the premiums before returning them. The deduction would be based on how long the car has been driven and what it would cost to cover the car under the Road Traffic Act for that period.

Social or business use?

Your policy will state the use you can put your car to. If the policy covers you for social, domestic and pleasure purposes and you use it for business you are violating the terms of the policy and may find that you are not covered. Insurers tend to divide use of cars into classes. Class 1 has the lowest premium, Class 3 has the highest. Class 1 is relevant if you use the car for social, domestic and pleasure purposes and if you use it, as a policyholder, for business. The premium could be 30% more in Class 2 if the business use is extended to other persons such as a partner or employer. The premium could be 60% more in Class 3 if business use includes commercial travellers and sales representatives.

Can you give lifts?

It is possible to give lifts and for cars seating up to eight passengers motor insurers have agreed that payments by passengers towards your **running costs** will not be treated as 'hiring' or 'hire or reward' for insurance purposes. This will not affect your policy. However, such an agreement does not apply if you make a business out of carrying such passengers or profit from the payments.

How much does motor insurance cost?

The premium on motor insurance depends on your age, occupation and driving record. If you want to pay low motor premiums then it is not a good idea to be under the age of 25 or above 70. If you are too young you are considered too immature by insurance companies and may find you are paying more premiums. If you are over 70 you may have difficulty in finding a new insurer. If you are **over 75** insurers may ask for a **doctor's certificate** every year or ask you to sign a declaration of health before continuing with the cover. Your occupation will also make difference to what you pay. Teachers, office workers, employees of banks or insurance companies and the police may acquire preferential rates, however, if you are a journalist, jockey, croupier or belong to a band you may have to pay more. If you happen to be a teacher by day, but a band leader in your spare time you may find that your part-time occupation is increasing your premiums. In other words, the more 'adventurous' your occupation, the higher the premiums you are often asked to pay.

You can also expect to pay more if you have just acquired a license or if you have a poor driving record. If you have a number of motoring convictions then your premiums may be increased according to the motoring points you have accumulated. A young or new driver with a number of convictions may find it difficult to get insurance at a reasonable price. Some companies may only insure him for three months at a time. However, some insurers do specialise in such risks.

Additionally, your other considerations will have an effect on the amount of premium you will pay.

Car types

Insurers group cars into categories ranging from minis to porsches and jaguars. The mini is the cheapest to insure, the porsche one of the most expensive. In some cases the age of your car will also affect premiums and the older the car the less the premium. If the car is between four to six years old you may get 7½% off on the premium, if it is seven years old, 15% off. A mini more than seven years old has one of the lowest premiums.

Location

Where you live and whether your car is in a **garage** or on the road will affect how much premium you pay. Insurers have divided the country into several areas and if you live in a rural area or one of the offshore islands where traffic density is supposed to be low you will pay less. If you live in an **inner city area** of London you may pay some of the highest premiums in the land. But such classifications vary considerably between insurance companies. One insurance company may rate a London suburb which is three or four miles from the centre as an outer area attracting lower premiums, another may rate it as part of central London attracting the highest premiums. So it is wise to shop around to find the best bargain.

The number of drivers you have

The fewer drivers you have the lower the premiums. If you want comprehensive cover to enable any driver to use your car then you are likely to be paying quite high premiums. If you limit the driving to **yourself and your spouse** you could receive a discount. If the insurance only covers you you may find that you are getting quite a big discount. Discount can vary between 7½% to 12½ %.

The nature of the cover

Comprehensive cover will cost more than third party, fire and theft and that in turn more than just third party. Insurance companies will ask you to fill in a fairly detailed proposal form which will ask you all sorts of questions that may help them decide on the above factors.

No-claims bonus

Basically, this is meant to provide an **incentive** to those who do not make claims on insurance companies when they damage their cars. The scale of such bonuses varies from 25% for one year without a claim to 60% or 65% for five years without a claim. The no-claims bonus is more like a snakes and ladders game. If, in any one year, you make a claim you move back two steps and will find that the bonus is reduced and the premium is higher when you come to renew your policy.

You can protect your no-claims bonus. A **protected no-claims** generally means that if you make a certain number of claims within a certain period of time you will not lose your no-claims bonus. This again will vary from insurer to insurer. For some companies it could mean two claims in any three-year period, or five-year period. Some insurers will openly tell you how many claims you can make, others are more secretive. In order to obtain protected no-claims bonus you must be between the ages 25 to 65, prove that you have not made a claim for the last five years and be free from motoring convictions. It is possible that you may have to pay an extra 6% or 10% in premiums for this protection.If you are transferring insurers and have a no-claims bonus then you can get a discount from the new insurers. The broker who is handling your insurance will deal with such matters.

Excess

Most motor insurance policies will expect you to pay an excess. So if you have an accident where the insurance company is meeting the claim you may still be required to pay for an excess of £50. It is useful to agree to pay such an excess because it can help reduce your premium by between 7% and 10%. Young drivers under 25 may have to pay a compulsory excess of between £100 and £150. If you come into this category then do not take the voluntary excess, because you will have a compulsory excess in any case.

Making a claim

Car insurance is not something you want to make a claim on. But what happens when you do have to make claims? Of the 11 million cars insured, some two and a half million owners make a claim every year – that is **one car in five**. So there is a chance that you may have to make a claim.

After an accident your first concern must be to make sure that people are safe and that the injured are being looked after. After that what should you do? *Crunch* is a very useful guide from the **Association of British Insurers** on what you should do after an accident. Some guidelines are summarised here.

1 Obtain name(s) and address(es) of other driver(s) involved.
2 Note their vehicle registration number(s) and make of vehicle.
3 Ask for the name of their insurers and their policy or certificate number.
4 Note name(s) and address(es) of independent witnesses and make a rough diagram of the accident.
5 If anybody is injured produce your certificate of insurance. If you do not give this information at the scene of the accident produce it for the police as soon as possible and not later than 24 hours after the accident. If there is an injury to any person or animal or damage to another vehicle or other property, give your name and the address of the owner of the vehicle you are driving and its registration number to anyone who has reasonable grounds for wanting them.
6 Report to your insurers any statement made at the scene of the accident by any of the parties. Do not discuss whose fault it was as this may create difficulties for your insurers in the handling of your claim.
7 Inform your insurers as soon as possible even if you do not intend to make a claim. This is a condition of your policy.
8 Complete the insurers accident report form and include any additional relevant information not given in answer to direct questions.

Your next step will be to get your car repaired and then see how this affects your policy and the no-claims bonus.

Repairs

As far as repairs are concerned you can take your car to any garage of your choice. But, obviously, it is advisable to take it to a competent garage. You may have to have your car towed from the place of accident to the garage and here, belonging to the **AA** or the **RAC** may be a help. You should get your garage to provide an estimate which you should send as soon as possible to the insurer. The insurer will check this estimate and, depending on the damage, send an engineer to the garage to check the car. Once he has submitted his report and the insurance company has authorised the repairs you can go ahead with getting your car back into shape. Respraying the car is one contentious area that is worth settling right at the start. Is the insurer expecting you to pay for the re-spraying?

When the garage presents his bill pay the excess that you have agreed on your policy and the rest will be met by the insurance company. This excess should be paid irrespective of who is to blame for the accident and whether you intend to claim from the other party to the accident. Your insurers may also require you to pay a portion of the cost of the repairs if the vehicle is being put in a better condition than before the accident, eg, a partly worn tyre or battery replaced by a new one. The cost of getting the car back to you is normally paid by most insurers. So, if the accident happened in Grantham and you are in London you can obtain the cost of a single train ticket from London to Grantham.

What if the car is a total loss?

If the car is a wreck the insurance company will generally offer what they call a total loss settlement: the current market price for the car in the condition it was at the time of the crash (which you can check in *Glass's Guide to Used Cars*). However, claims for write-offs are often difficult and have proved a headache to the Ombudsman who, in his report for 1982, said:

'There is sometimes an arrangement between insurance companies and scrap merchants for the disposal of written-off cars which can work to the advantage of all concerned. However, such arrangements are always open to abuse and two such cases have been brought to my attention, one where a car which had been immersed in sea water was turned into a runner before the owner had agreed a settlement and another where an owner went to the garage to collect some property left in the car and found that the wheels and various other parts had already disappeared. I am quite satisfied that insurance companies are not parties to activity of this kind and indeed are victims as much as the aggrieved car owners. Nevertheless, a company which has undertaken to look after the wreck is responsible for it and if there has been any such conversion I am bound to treat the matter on the basis of damages for conversion rather than on the basis of reimbursement of the market value of the car. This is because at the end of the day the policyholder has the right to strike a bargain with the company involving his keeping the scrap. Conversion may have deprived him of that right.'

Despite the warnings issued by the Ombudsman that the motor claims department of companies should be vigilant against this abuse, not much action seems to have taken place to enforce a rule of vigilance.

What you need to watch out for in such situations is that between the time of the accident and the insurer deciding that the claim can be met on the basis that the car is a write-off, many months may lapse. What is the legal position of the property? This is important if we follow an example of what might happen if the insurance company does not keep a tight grip on events. For example, in February you have an accident. In July the car is moved to 'free storage' which means a scrap yard where, without your knowledge, the car is cannibalised and sold. In November the insurance company finally decides that they cannot meet the accident damages claim since three of the tyres were bald and contributed materially to the accident. In such a situation as the Insurance Ombudsman has pointed out, 'the insurer is likely to find that he will have to pay in damage for conversion of the car, the salvage value at the time of conversion, although he has refused to make any payment under the policy'.

Retrospective ownership

The point is, that in such situations, ownership passes retrospectively. If, at the end of the day, the insurance company meets the claim there is no problem. If it does not then you have problems similar to the one we have seen. The Ombudsman's suggestion is that if there is any likelihood of the claim not being met then the decision whether to meet the claim or not must be taken before the car is moved to the scrap yard. If the decision has to be postponed the policyholder must be informed beforehand and encouraged to consent to any such move. If the car has to be moved to the scrapyard the scrap merchant must be told that the car cannot be cannibalised or sold until he is officially notified in writing. It might be a good idea to have a photograph of the car at the time of the removal.

It is worth noting the Ombudsman conclusion's on this subject in his report for 1987: 'The essential point is that unless ultimate payment is certain, with its retrospective transfer of ownership to the insurer, nothing must be done which is, in the technical phrase, "inconsistent with the policyholder's ownership of the vehicle". This problem arises more often than most insurers think'.

Market value and economic value

What happens if the repairs cost less than the pre-accident market value? According to the 1987 Insurance Ombudsman report: 'No insurer may take the salvage value of a damaged motor car into account if the repairs cost less than the pre-accident market value. If the cost of repairs will exceed the market value, salvage value may properly be taken into account because ownership of the salvage passes to the insurer who pays on total loss basis. In other words, market value not economic value marks the point of no return, whatever the industry practice may be. Where the repairs amount to less than the market value, the insurer has no proprietary interest whatever in the salvage and must not try and impose a settlement by way of an economic write-off on any claimant'.

What often tends to happen is that when the cost of repairs is estimated to be only slightly less than the market value the insurance company will say it is an **economic total loss**. There is nothing to stop the insurance company from offering to pay market value for the salvage but as the Ombudsman points out the injustice lies in trying to deny the owner the right to keep his car. In fact, the vast majority of car owners who are faced with repairs lasting several weeks would no doubt prefer a cash settlement for the market value and invest it in a replacement vehicle, but the enthusiast must be catered for if injustice is to be avoided. If such a person wants to repair his car and repairs cost less than the market value, the only options for the insurer under normal current policy wording are to have the repairs done or to pay their estimated cost and let the owner have them done. If your car is a write-off you can make a third party claim against the company with whom the person held responsible for the accident was insured.

Minor repairs

In most comprehensive policies claims for broken windscreen or paintwork scratched owing to breakage will not affect the no-claims bonus. In many cases you can also get it replaced or repaired and the cost reimbursed without having to check with your insurer.

How do claims affect your no-claims bonus?

Nothing concerns motorists more than the effect of an accident on a claim bonus. In many cases a motorist who is at fault will prefer to settle a claim privately rather than involve his insurance company. But remember, you are required to notify your insurance company whether you make a claim or not. Even if the other party offers to make a private settlement always get their name and address, and the name of their insurance company, address and other details we discussed earlier. If you are not making a claim against your insurance company make sure when filling in the claim form or the **motor accident form** to write the report only in bold letters or in suitably coloured ink. Sometimes the forms have a box which you can tick to indicate that you are reporting an accident, not making a claim.

However, as the Insurance Ombudsman has pointed out, there is still a tendency to treat any accident report as an automatic claim. The insurance company should not do anything that would prejudice your no-claims bonus, but they often do. Claims managers of insurance companies will look critically at their own policyholder's accident report but not the claims by a third party against their own policyholder. The result, says the Ombudsman is that 'many claims managers seem to find it easier to yield to pressure from third parties or their insurers and so pay doubtful claims, than to resist those claims and test the statements. Perhaps they are more frightened of the prospect of paying costs if they resist then they are of the righteous wrath of their own policyholders whose no-claims discount have been reduced and whose plans to sue in the small claims court for uninsured losses they may have severely prejudiced'. If your insurer makes a third party payment even without admitting liability the very fact of such a payment can prejudice your chances of making a claim for uninsured losses by encouraging the third party's to defend a claim where they might otherwise have settled.

The problem is that motor accidents are traumatic affairs where both parties can often believe they are right and even the independent witness can make mistakes. The point is well stated by the Insurance Ombudsman in his 1987 report: 'It is well known that according to the version given to their respective insurance companies, each was stationary on his side of the road when the other ran into him. This is, of course, a standard joke, but there is a grain of truth in it. The trauma of collision, whether you are a driver or a passenger has a profound effect on your ability to recollect accurately what happened. . . . Even the highly regarded "independent" witness can err. Often his attention is only drawn to the accident by the noise of the crash and he cheerfully gives evidence of what he thinks happened as against what he saw. He can occasionally be deceived. The driver who slightly overshoots the red light and reverses into the car behind may, to the passer-by, who only hears the noise, look like the innocent party in a standard traffic-light crash'.

Yet in such cases where there is confusion and conflict, claim managers of insurance companies can often give their own policyholder a hard time when it comes to third party claims. So, beware.

Knock-for-knock

This is an agreement between two insurance companies that when two vehicles have been in collision each company pays for the damage to the car it has insured provided, of course, that the policy fully covers the damage risk. This is done regardless of liability and speeds up authorising of repair work and reduces the administrative costs. This should not normally affect your no-claims bonus if you can obtain full recovery of your claim from the other party involved in the accident. But since an accident is rarely one person's fault your no-claims bonus most likely will be affected. However, if you have a long history of no-claims then you may get by with a reduction. One problem is that insurance companies do not tell you that they are going to settle under a knock-for-knock agreement.

How can you protect your no-claims bonus?

If you are convinced that you are not to blame make sure you collect and present to the insurance company all the evidence to support your contention. The crucial question is whether the **police** are likely to prosecute the other driver. If so, it strengthens your case and you should mention this on the accident form. If they are not going to prosecute perhaps because the car that collided with you was stolen and the driver cannot be found, then no amount of righteous indignation will help your no-claims bonus. If you can persuade the other driver to pay for your uninsured loss then this would be taken as evidence by your insurers that the other driver was at fault.

Uninsured losses

These are losses which are not covered even by a comprehensive policy and include such expenses as:

- The excess you have to pay
- Out-of-pocket expenses
- Treatment or transport for injury
- Compensation for personal injury
- Loss of earnings because of time off from work
- Cost of alternative transport to work or hire of car while your car is out of action.

Third party claims made by you

You should send your claim for uninsured losses to the third party by recorded delivery. He will probably pass it to his insurers and the whole question of establishing the claim will begin. If you succeed there is nothing to worry about but you may find that by this time you have acquired a few grey hairs for it can take a long time. You could threaten legal action against the third party and, for any amounts under £500, you can claim through the **county court's 'small claims'** procedure. For larger amounts, or for a claim for serious personal injury you may have to call in a **solicitor**. But if you hold a third party entirely to blame, in order to preserve your no-claims bonus you should pursue the claim, not involve your insurer. If you do that it becomes a claim on your insurance policy and could affect your no-claims bonus.

Third party claims made against you

If you receive such a claim send it straight to your insurer or if you are dealing with a broker send it to him together with your report of the accident and any witnesses' statements that you may have. All further correspondence should be passed unanswered to your insurers, but keep a copy of such letters and a record of how the claim is proceeding. Of course, you could deal with the other person's claim yourself.

Injuries

As we have seen, the law requires that you have minimum insurance to cover injury to another person – a passenger in your car, a pedestrian, another driver for which you are liable. You should send the injured person's claim to your insurers.

If you have been injured under a comprehensive policy you should be covered and can claim under the **personal accident** section for a lump sum payment. This payment will not be affected by the fact that the accident was your fault. Such payments, be they death, or loss of sight, or loss of eyes or of limbs is generally limited to £2,500 for each category. You may find that doctors charge for emergency medical assistance at the roadside and so do hospitals for emergency treatment. These fees will be paid by the insurer. If the bill comes to you, pay first and then have them reimbursed by the insurer. Most comprehensive policies also pay medical expenses to persons injured in your car with a limit of £50 or £100 per person.

What happens if your car is stolen?

You should first notify the police and then tell your insurer. You should be prepared to wait for a few days since many cars are taken for joy-rides or for criminal purposes and are often abandoned after a few days. Insurers generally wait for a few weeks before paying out on a stolen car. What the insurer will offer is on a total loss basis. Should the car be recovered it will became the property of the insurer and you would have to negotiate if you want to buy it back. However, if the insurers say you can have your car back, provided you return the claim money, you are not required to accept his proposal.

It is worth nothing that you cannot claim theft if you sell your car privately and hand over the title and possession of the car to someone who turns out to be a confidence trickster who has probably given you a stolen cheque or a duff bank draft.

What happens if possessions are taken from your car?

Here again you should report the theft to the police and then your insurance company. Under a comprehensive policy you are protected against loss or damage to rugs, clothing and personal belongings in the car, usually to a limit of £50 or £100. This does not apply to fitted car radios or cassette players which are considered part of the car and covered in full.

What you have to decide is whether you should claim under a motor car policy, or perhaps, use the household insurance policy you have. If you have an all-risks household policy then you can recover the full amount of the value of the goods lost. Additionally, claiming against a motor insurance policy will affect your no-claims bonus. If you do not have an all risks policy you could claim under a household contents policy but you may only get back 15% of the value of what you have lost.

Insuring car telephones

By 1990 there may be half a million car telephones in use. Those of us who do not have one may regard these as unnecessary but there is no doubt a great many people do have such telephones and if you have one you ought to think about insuring it.

There are three types of cellular telephones: mobiles, which are permanently fitted to a car; transportables, which require a fairly substantial battery pack and portables, which are normally powered by a small battery that fits inside the equipment. Insurance does not come cheap and many insurance companies refuse outright to insure them.

To insure your car telephone you have to consider whether to tack them on to your motor policy or to the all risks section of a home contents policy. If the carphone is fixed to the car then it may be considered part and parcel of the car and covered just like any other part of the vehicle. However, a claim will mean a loss of the no-claims bonus which in turn could lead to a substantial increase in premiums when the policy comes up for renewal. If the car phone is transportable or portable it will be classed along with rugs, clothing and other personal possessions. This means that in the event of a loss or damage you are only likely to get about £100. A better bet would be to include it in the all risks section of your household contents policy, but you will have to list it as a specified valuable and this could mean paying a substantial premium.

You can cover breakdown of car telephones but you will need specialist policies for these and subsequently you will have to pay quite heavy premiums. Breakdown cover costs range from £65 for in-car fixed models for one year or £80 for transportables and portables to £240 for four years for the in-car version or £290 for the carry-around models.

There is generally an agreement between insurers that in a

claim concerning household or all-risks policy, they will not seek a contribution from the motor insurers. So this should protect your no-claims bonus.

Motor cycle insurance

In many ways this is very similar to motor car insurance. The compulsory Road Traffic Act requirements are the same and you can obtain the same third party only, third party fire and theft and comprehensive cover. In the traditional type of motor cycle policy, also known as specified cycle policy, the proposal forms are very similar to that for cars except that no details are required for business use. Cover is limited to the policyholder and therefore name and full details are required of any person named as **additional rider**.

You can get a special motor cycle policy called **Motor Cycle Rider Policy**. When it was introduced in 1970 it was a departure from traditional policy since it provides full cover on any motor cycle owned by, or ridden by, the policyholder provided that it is not a cycle belonging to his employer. The cycle has to be within the cubic capacity limit shown on the policy. But on such policies you cannot get a no-claims bonus. The proposal form for these are very simple requiring only the policyholder's name, address, age, details of previous insurance, motoring convictions, accidents, and any physical or mental infirmities.

Motor cycle policies do not normally include theft of accessories or spare parts unless the motor cycle is stolen as well. Nor can you claim for loss of coats, any personal belongings or gear. Whilst liability to passengers is covered there is no personal accident cover for the insured driver or rider. Premium is based on the cubic capacity of the bike, the length of time you have owned it and your age. Since it is assumed that motor cycles attract the young, if you are over 25 you can acquire considerably lower premiums. Where you live will also affect premiums. You can take out policies that cover periods of less than a year and you then pay a certain percentage.

Caravans

Nearly all motor car policies give you Road Traffic Act or third party cover for towing caravans provided that your caravan is properly attached to your car – but check the policy to make sure. However, aside from third party cover, if the caravan is attached to the car, no other section of your motor policy extends to it. Even if you have comprehensive cover this will not cover you for any accidental damage to the caravan while it is being towed or while it is on site. Therefore, if while you are driving your caravan sways out and hits an oncoming car you may be covered by your usual car policy but not for any damage that your caravan has suffered.

In such an instance you will need a **specific caravan policy** or you could have it covered as part of your household contents or sports equipment policy. A caravan policy will cover you for loss or damage to the caravan and its equipment and fittings. If your caravan is a total loss then you would be compensated for what it has been insured for. This would be based on *Glass's Guide to Caravan Values*. If you have improved the caravan make sure your sum insured reflects this. In some cases if your caravan is less than a year old you may get new for old insurance. But if it is more than 10 years old you may get nothing.

You must check to see whether you are insured when the caravan is being towed. The policy should allow you to take the caravan to the nearest repairer and following repairs return to your home address. If you have to arrange for alternative accommodation while the caravan is being repaired this may be provided for.

Your normal household policies may cover possessions in the caravan but check to see how extensive this cover is. Does it extend to television, video, and audio equipment which you want in a caravan? You may need an optional extension to cover personal possessions in the caravan. Many caravan policies cover you for between a month and 60 days if you take it abroad. But the caravan must be shown on the car's green card when you take it out of this country.

Motoring abroad

If you want to drive abroad, that is outside the UK, Channel Islands and the Isle of Man, you will be well advised to tell your insurers. Your normal UK car policy will automatically provide the minimum legal cover required in all EEC countries plus Austria, Czechoslovakia, the German Democratic Republic, Finland, Hungary, Norway, Sweden and Switzerland. But that is only the minimum cover and should you have an accident this will hardly be enough.

What you should do once you have decided on your holiday is to notify your insurance company or broker and you will be issued with a **green card** which is an International Motor Insurance Certificate. This will extend your UK cover to the EEC and the other countries mentioned as well as Bulgaria, Iceland, Iran, Iraq, Israel, Morocco, Poland, Portugal, Rumania, Spain, Tunisia and Yugoslavia. In the countries we have just listed if you do not have a green card you will have to take out **local insurance** at short term rates. Being in possession of a green card does not mean that your policy has been extended to supply the same cover in these countries as in the UK. You have to ask your insurer to provide this. You may find that your insurer may not be willing to provide the same UK cover to all the countries we have just listed. You ought to clarify the situation before you travel. What you need to inform your insurance company is the details of the car you are driving, the countries you are visiting and the period of your travel. If you are taking a caravan or towing any vehicle mention that as well.

You will probably be charged a flat fee for the green card, or according to the type of car you are driving. The average cost of a green card is between £10 and £20 for a period of one month. At double the cost you can get a separate package which includes breakdown, recovery assistance and a combined continental claims service. Make sure you sign the green card before travel to make it effective.

If you are involved in an accident in any of the countries mentioned on the green card you should contact the local **Green Card Bureau** to report the accident. Also, report accidents to your insurance company's local representatives and to your insurance company on your return. In most western European countries, particularly France, Belgium and Italy a form called the **Constat Amiable** is used. This is a standardised **European Accident Statement** which enables drivers to exchange facts while events are still fresh in their minds. Your insurer will issue you with an English version and the English translation closely follows the continental format. This makes it easy to fill in the continental form.

If your car is a total loss or is stolen you may be required by the government of the country in which you are visiting to pay import duty. You can extend your UK policy to cover this.

If you are driving through Spain then get a **Fianza** – a bail bond. The Spanish legal system allows the authorities there to detain you and/or your car following an accident unless a deposit is made against the possibility of your being found responsible for the accident. The bond will act as a surety to supplement the minimum level of cover required by law. You may obtain it free with the green card or pay a little extra for it.

You can get a fairly good vehicle breakdown insurance service. This package (which some insurers provide with the green card) will enable you to get your vehicle back to the UK, provide an allowance to enable you to hire a car or a chauffeur if the only driver is ill, repatriate the passengers, and pay for fares to continue the journey, or return to the UK. Transport of spare parts, the cost of towing the vehicle to the nearest garage, hotel expenses abroad while you wait and bail bonds for Spain are also catered for. Some of these sections may have a monetary limit on how much you can secure. The cost of such policies will depend on the age of the car. Usually a car more than 10 years old is unlikely to get cover. Cover of this nature may double the green card cost to between £20 and £30 for a month's cover.

Alternatively, a similar policy can be taken out with companies such as Mondial which is used by the insurers to provide you this service. Such schemes also supply a 24-hour telephone number which you can ring and, if necessary, reverse the charges. Make sure you have this number on you before you set out on your travels. This telephone number may be in the UK or in the country you are driving through. Companies that provide such service pride themselves on the fact that once you have made the call they respond very quickly. You will, of course, have to help by providing details about your car, where the vehicle is, and the nature and extent of the damage.

Such policies have a condition that your vehicle has been regularly serviced in accordance with a manufacturer's warranty and if it has not then you may find that you are required to meet the cost of the repairs. As an incentive to get you to buy their cars certain car **manufacturers** provide such 24-hour emergency service as part of a new car package.

Car hire in the USA and Canada

In recent years fly-drive holidays in the USA and Canada have become very popular. However, in the USA road traffic legislation is a matter for individual states. This means motor insurance varies from state to state, some states do not have any compulsory motor insurance and the states that do have them tend to have very low limits from as low as £5,000. In an accident you will be held personally liable for any claim for injury or damage over this limit.

Since the standard travel insurance excludes liability arising from use of vehicles, tour operators use car companies who provide third party liability insurance well above the variable statutory minimum but even such limits are low compared with court awards. It is common for tour operators to offer **excess liability insurances** to provide for adequate protection.

The insurance provides cover against third party and passenger liability. This is compensation for injury which cannot be recovered because the other motorist is either uninsured or underinsured, or cannot be traced. The basic premium is $35 per vehicle for four drivers for a limit of $1 million and $45 for higher limits. If the driver is under 25 years old then the premiums may increase. You can get this supplementary cover even if you do not hire a car through a fly-drive operator but at an increased cost. You must purchase such insurance before you leave the UK.

10 Insurance for sports

Sport may be good for you and it is enjoyed by millions but whilst pursuing your favourite sports you could either injure yourself or cause others harm and for this reason you do need some form of insurance to protect yourself. Professional bodies which organise sports have a variety of insurance needs and these are somewhat outside the scope of this book. Here we are concerned with the amateur pursuing sports for relaxation and pleasure. As we all grow conscious of our health and fitness so we participate more in sports for recreation and fun. This makes the need for insurance cover all the more important.

Sports insurance needs to cover:

- **Public liability** which may arise as a result of your sporting actions causing death or injury to others or damage to their property
- Loss of **sporting equipment**
- **Personal accident** to yourself as a result of sports activities
- Loss of **personal effects**.

Where to obtain sports insurance

Generally, much of the sporting cover you need can be arranged through existing policies, or by a suitable extension. Most **household contents policies** would cover public liability up to half a million pounds or a £1 million. This will cover public liability that involves nearly all sports apart from those involving aircraft, motorcars or sail-powered water craft. Such policies are also restricted to the UK only. Some of these policies may exclude guns. But if you are an archer and instead of hitting the bull's eye you hit someone else you should be covered by the public liability section of your household contents policy.

Cover for the physical sports equipment, can be included within the **all risks cover** but you may have to specify the equipment. This is wider than the normal household contents policy because cover is available outside the home. All risks would exclude items associated with the normal use of the equipment, like the breakage of strings on rackets, etc.

Personal accident cover may also be included under household insurance but you may find that its normal range has to be extended to cover sports, particularly if you pursue a hazardous sport. What you are likely to find is that the cost will depend on the sort of sports you are indulging in. If you are a golfer or a squash player then you are likely to be covered at basic rates. But if you are a mountaineer and are looking to get cover for yourself and your tent pitched at 14,000 foot up the Himalayas then this section of the household policy is clearly inadequate. The reasons for this are that you are likely to need medical cover and as you are abroad you will need a host of other covers.

If you belong to an association or club then you may find it very useful to obtain group personal accident policy. For non-hazardous sports premiums are low. Claims on such policies are few, profits are high and insurers often give deep discounts to attract business. There is a difference in premiums for death in capital sums cover and for weekly benefits. If you are seeking weekly benefits then you may have to pay higher premiums.

Types of cover available

To cater for individual sports there are a variety of special insurances. Thus, an angler package scheme aimed at all amateur coarse, game or seashore anglers provides all risks cover for equipment plus personal accident and public liability cover. Similar schemes are available in most other sports. The *1987 Insurance Buyers Guide* which provides a handy list of most insurance policies on the market lists 69 insurance policies available to the sportsman ranging from athletics to canoeing to lacrosse and windsurfing. In addition to specialised insurance policies for individual sports you can also find policies that cover most sports. There are policies available which cover you for personal accident to suit **individual sporting requirements** catering for sports such as football, rugby and cricket. Dental cover may also be available.

Personal accident policies are also available for amateur clubs which pay weekly benefits. In high risk sports such as parachutists (including free fall), jockeys, boxers and stuntmen there are special high risk personal accident and sickness schemes. One insurance company offers a package policy which provides personal accident cover including limited sickness, loss of speech/hearing, disappearance and hijack. Most sports, including water sports are included.

A cover for soft-tissue medical treatment is also available. Under this policy cover is provided for the cost of **outpatient treatment** for soft-tissue injuries as a result of participating in any organised amateur sport. It provides the cost of fees payable to doctors and physiotherapists for the diagnosis and treatment given at the time of the diagnosis and physiotherapy and manipulative treatment of soft-tissue injuries.

One Lloyd's broker provides a Sportsmen's and Women's Personal Accident Scheme which covers against death, dismemberment, disablement, weekly indemnity and medical expenses following accident and sickness. Every sport is covered including overseas sports travel.

If you run a sports club then you should consider taking out an all risk cover for amateur **sports equipment**. Most sports equipment will be covered though certain types may be excluded. You can also get a personal accident scheme for sports and social clubs which provides composite cover for amateur risks of the popular sports and such activities as darts, clay pigeon shooting, drama classes, dance classes, etc. You can get what is called overall 'block' cover to include public liability cover for cups, trophies, etc.

Messing about in boats

If you like messing about in boats and it is a large boat that takes your fancy then you must consider **marine insurance**. This is specialised and here you will be introduced to new terms and jargon. A small craft insurance will suffice for a boat that is not more than five metres long and if power driven has a maximum speed of 17 knots. As a general rule, a small boat is one you can pick up out of the water and store say, in your backyard; a large boat, requiring specialised marine insurance, is not easily removed from its natural surroundings. However, if you charge to take people out on the boat, even if it is for fishing trips or sightseeing then you have to insure in the commercial marine category.

Most brokers provide insurance for boats but you may obtain cheaper rates if you belong to **sailing clubs**. You may find that a household contents policy will insure small boats as an extension to your policy but this may not be cheap. How much you pay will depend on how often the boat is in the water and ready for use and where you store it when you do not use it. You could insure it for just one month in a year, if that is all you use it for, and you may be able to reduce premiums by paying a voluntary excess of about £25.

There are no-claims bonuses and the bigger the boat the larger the no-claims bonus. Up to 20% is common and there is at least one scheme, underwritten by Lloyds, where the top rate of bonus after four claim-free years is 40%. This is for craft valued at between £10,000 and £100,000.

What does boat insurance cover?

You can insure for:

- **Loss or damage** to the boat, along with its tackle, fitting and equipment provided it is caused by accidental external means
- **Stress** due to weather
- Stranding, sinking or collision
- Malicious acts causing **damage** to your boat
- **Theft** of boat or of gear and equipment though for that you need forcible entry
- **Fire**, lightning and explosion
- Breaking of the **propellor shaft**
- The **outboard motor** dropping overboard
- **Salvage** charges
- **Third party** liabilities up to £250,000 or some up to £500,000. Such third party damage could involve damage to piers, docks, jetties, claims made by passengers for death or bodily injuries, damage to their property and legal costs incurred
- Cover for crew. Note that third party liability does not cover employees so if you pay your crew you need separate cover for them.

Small boats cover has many exclusions and wear and tear, depreciation, war and riots, etc, are not covered. Outboard motors are very popular with thieves and insurers may say that a motor must be locked in a secure place when not in use. It must not be left on the transom of the boat and you must keep the serial number. If you race the boat then the extent of your cover may be reduced whilst racing.

One area where boat insurance differs from motor insurance is that there is **no great saving in restricting it to third party**. There is a serious risk that if somebody else damages your boat you may not be able to make a full recovery because he will be able to claim 'limitation of liability', leaving you to foot the bill for repairs.

For a long time it was not possible to get **warranty insurance** for boats, so there was nothing you could do if the mast fell, the propellor dropped off or a large crack appeared in the hull. But now warranty insurance for boats is available. It is rather similar to warranty insurance for secondhand cars. New boats come with a manufacturer's warranty valid for a year, which can be extended for a second year. This is also available for second hand boats. It provides cover against structural failure of the hull and spares and mechanical failure of the engine and steering gear for 12 months from the date of purchase in the case of secondhand boats. These boats must be less than six years old. A warranty is granted on the basis of a survey and any defects picked up on the survey are excluded unless they are put right and passed by the surveyor.

One thing worth noting is that if you hire a sail boat whilst on holiday your holiday insurance will not cover you for public liability. So if the skeg of the sail boat – the fin at the back of the sail boat – runs over a swimmer cutting him or her you will not be covered. You may have assumed that the person hiring the sail boat has that cover but this assumption may turn out to be wrong. In such a case you will be liable. So check to see how you are covered.

11 Insurance for the organiser

If you are an organiser of an event, be it a garden fête, a charity evening, or even a sporting occasion you have some responsibility to make sure you have adequate insurance cover. As a minimum you ought to have public and products liability. **Public liability** will cover you if members of the public suffer death, injury or loss to their property as a result of the event you have organised. **Product liability** will take care of any claims arising from food and drinks that you may be serving during the event.

If this is a one-off event then you need only take out a single insurance policy, if it is an annual event you may think of suitable annual cover. Generally, such events are organised by a committee and it would be advisable for the policy to have an extension so that member to member liability is included. This is important because when people form a committee to organise an event they acquire a quasi-legal status somewhere between the identity of the individual and that of a company. Thus, **committee members** have a liability as a committee over and above their individual liability. So, for instance, if a member of the committee were to accidentally injure another he could sue the other member individually or the committee collectively. The collective insurance cover should include liability for each member to every other member.

But while this provides minimum protection the organiser should also consider some form of **property insurance** to protect equipment hired.

Pluvius insurance

Rain is a cruel but unavoidable part of the English summer and organisers of summer fêtes, gymkhanas, garden parties, sports days and weddings all know the havoc rain can play.

The answer is pluvius insurance. Basically, it provides organisers with a fixed sum should a certain amount of rain fall during a specified period. Rainfall measurements are taken at a number of places throughout the country by the 5,000 member **British Rainfall Organisation** and the rainfall stipulations in a policy vary according to the location and the season.

The cost of pluvius depends on:

- The time of the year—July and August are usually wetter than May, June and September
- Geographical location
- The rainfall measurement chosen
- The number of hours cover needed.

It is advisable to arrange cover to start well before the event opens. Rain insurance should start a couple of hours before the garden fête is to be opened since a downpour then may deter a lot of people from turning up. Additionally, whilst the sun may shine during the Mayor's speech there may be hardly anyone present since they were put off by the earlier downpour. It is actually rather difficult to get the timing right on this insurance. You could find that you have insured against rainfall between 11.30 am and 4.30 pm and it rains heavily until 11 am and clears. This could deter many people from coming to your fête but you will not be able to claim on the policy.

Pluvius premiums range from £8 to £14 per £100 of cover and rates have not altered in this country since 1952. Indeed, it is interesting to note that long spells of dry weather actually encourage people to take out such insurance. Eagle Star who lead the field in such insurance found that in the long summer of 1976 they wrote more pluvius insurance than at any other time.

12 Insurance for pets

Dogs and cats

If you have pets they may be involved in events which will cost you money. You can protect against that by taking out a separate policy for pets. Some cover just dogs and cats, others cover horses and all non-farm animals as well.

A policy for dogs or cats may provide:

Liability

Suppose, as happened recently, a car hit a boxer dog. The dog was unhurt, but the car was damaged to the extent of £450. If your dog caused such damage the policy could help you meet such costs.

Vet's fees

There are various limits ranging from £50 to £200 per dog or cat per incident in this section of the policy. Fees in connection with pregnancy or breeding are excluded, vet's travelling expenses are not met and nor is the cost of routine innoculation.

Loss or stealing

If the dog or cat is lost, or stolen, or strays, the cost incurred in trying to get it back, again up to a limit, is met.

Death

If the animal dies or has to be killed by the vet for humane reasons you will get the market value or purchase price. However, some policies will not insure a cat's life and some pay a maximum amount on death.

Valuable animals

If your animal is worth more than £100 you may have to provide a certificate from the veterinary surgeon certifying the condition of the pet.

Horses and ponies

You can insure ponies or horses you keep either on the same policy as for a dog or a separate one. Premium is based on the sum insured and the use of the animal. You have to pay more if you use the horse for point-to-point races. The basic cover is for the animal's death and the damage it may do to people or their property with a specified limit of £500,000 or £100,000. The policy can be extended to cover vet's fees and theft or straying.

Exotic pets

You can get other types of insurance to cover more exotic pets. There are Lloyd's policies for killer whales, alligators and other such familiar friends of man. In many cases, you will find that such policies are not all that necessary. In the majority of cases liability involving animals can probably be met through the cover provided by household contents policy. But if you have unusual pets then obviously some sort of specialised cover is worth looking at.

13 Other insurances

There are many other insurance policies you can have and here we look at some of the more interesting ones.

What if your marriage does not work?

One in three marriages end in divorce so the chances of your marriage not working is quite high. 'Marriage insurance' cover underwrites maintenance payments and joint-earnings against illness, disability, redundancy, unfair dismissal or legal moves for lower payments. The policy, devised by a firm of Lloyd's brokers, comes in two parts. The first is the **maintenance protection plan**. This can be used by the husband to insure against the income of his ex-wife falling in the event of illness, disability, redundancy or unfair dismissal which could mean a demand for higher maintenance from him. The other is a **maintenance payments plan** and is designed for a wife to insure against her ex-husband's earnings falling for any reason, including an application to the court for lower payments. There are no sex barriers and the policies are flexible. Either policy is available to either party in a divorce action and a first wife can insure her own earning capacity. The policies are not cheap but benefits can mean that a wife facing unfair dismissal or redundancy can acquire 75% of her earnings up to three years.

What if you have twins?

Your chance of having twins is considerably less than the chances of getting divorced. There is a one in 80 chance of having twins but this varies with the mother's age and the number of children she already has. If there are twins in either parents family it is even more likely that they will occur. Twins insurance will, for a modest premium, provide you extra cash on delivery to tide over the first difficult weeks. If you have triplets or quads the money is doubled. Money at this stage could prove most useful. If you are expecting just one child and then suddenly find that you have two or even three to look after, things could become quite complicated.

In order to obtain cover you will have to disclose whether there have been twins in the family going back to the grandparents' generation, whether a fertility drug or treatment is being taken in which case insurance may not be allowed and what the ultrasonic scan has shown. You must also own up if your doctor has ever told you that you are likely to have more than one baby or if there is anything else which could affect the outcome. You must provide a doctor's certificate showing the expected date of birth. Your proposal must be accepted and the premium paid at least six months before this. Even so, you cannot claim if your babies are born more than six weeks early and both must survive more than 24 hours.

The idea of the policy is to help with extra expenses around the time of birth, not with continuing cost of feeding, clothing and educating an extra child. So the maximum cover is £1,500, although most couples would probably be given around £600–£700. The minimum premium is £25. The cheapest premium is paid by mothers aged 25 or under, the rate then rises with age until age 40 after which twins are less likely. There is loading of 20% for women who already have three children.

14 Public Liability

Liability is one of those words which we often use without quite knowing what it means – or the wide ramifications of its use. For instance, we may say X is a liability, meaning he is more trouble than he is worth. Accountants speak of the liabilities of a business which include amounts due to trade creditors, loans borrowed from the bank, etc. Our leaders often speak of our moral liabilities, like our duties as a citizen, bringing up children or looking after aged parents.

The law has a more precise definition of liability and insurances which helps us cope with our legal responsibilities cover such definitions.

Strict liability

These are obligations imposed by law. If you occupy land then a judgment reached in 1868 declares that if you keep anything on the land that is likely to cause damage if it escapes, you are bound to prevent its escape or be responsible for the consequences of the escape even if you have not been guilty of negligence. Parliament also lays down certain statutory liability as, for instance, under the Occupiers Liability Act 1957.

Negligence

This is defined as something you have failed to do which, as a reasonable person guided by those considerations which govern our lives, you would be expected to do. Alternatively, it could be something you have done which, as a prudent and careful person, you may be expected not to do. Just because you are negligent does not mean you are liable. If somebody brings an action against he or she must also prove that you have:

- Had a duty of care towards that somebody
- That you breached that duty
- That as a result the somebody was injured or damaged in some way.

Negligent actions produce the most claims.

Nuisance

We all know the common use of the word. The law seeks to give it a shape. If you unlawfully disturb a person while he or she is enjoying his or her property or exercising his or her common rights you may commit a nuisance. You may be liable even if you have been reasonably careful. There can either be private nuisance where only the rights of an individual are affected, or public nuisance where the rights of the public are affected. In the latter case, however, a crime must be committed and special damage proved before civil action can be brought.

Trespass

In this case you commit an unlawful act with force and violence on the person or property of another. Merely being on someone else's land doesn't necessarily constitute tresspass.

Contractual liability

You may have agreed a written contract which increases your common law liability. If you employ people you may be liable for their actions or you may be liable for the actions committed while they are working for you. If you have hired independent contractors you are liable for what they do under contract.

We can draw two distinctions here. There is the liability for bodily injury or disease to employees and bodily injury or disease to third parties and loss or damage to their properties. The law makes no distinctions but insurance companies do. The first is covered by policies under employees liability, the second by policies under public liability or products liability. In recent years, however, there has been a tendency to issue combined liability policies covering all three risks.

The principles that govern liability insurance are the same as other insurances:

- Utmost good faith
- Insurable interest
- Indemnity where you are insured in respect of legal liabilities to pay compensation to third parties
- Subrogation where you may be liable for the negligence of an independent contractor you have employed.

There are several kinds of liability insurance:

Public liability insurance

This protects you against liability arising from commercial or business activity which results bodily injury to third parties or loss of or damage to their property.

Private liability insurance

This will cover you for liability arising in a personal and private capacity and excludes business activities. As far as personal liability insurance is concerned there are various ways it may arise. A canvasser could injure himself or herself as a result of falling on an uneven flagstone in the path to your front door, or a chimney pot could fall on a visitor's car in your driveway. Your son riding his bicycle might knock down a passer-by, or you might carelessly start a fire or cause a road accident by jay-walking. You could obtain separate liability insurance for this but in most cases household contents policy will cover you.

However, as we have noted, if you employ anyone your household contents policy will not cover you for any injury they may suffer while working for you. But liability for injury to domestic servants whilst working for you will be covered by a contents policy. What if you have taken on someone to do odd jobs in the garden? Say, in the course of what he is doing, he accidentally sets fire to your neighbour's hedge and fence. Your household contents policy will not cover the odd-jobbing gardener and you may have to take out liability insurance to cover his actions.

Products liability insurance

This relates to claims arising from injury to third parties or loss or damage to their property as a result of goods sold, supplied, repaired, serviced or tested by you. You can be liable either at common law through negligence, say, as a result of careless manufacture of an item or its packaging, distribution or storing. Or you may be liable on contract under the Sale of Goods Act 1893.

Employer's liability

This covers you as an employer against claims for damages brought by employees who, whilst working for you, may sustain bodily injury or illness which arises in connection with their employment.

Professional indemnity insurance

This covers you as a professional person against legal liability to compensate third parties who have sustained some injury, loss or damage due to your own professional negligence or that of your employees.

You can also secure cover of your copyrights, patents, design rights, trademarks or trade names. These are intangible rights which are often grouped together as industrial property rights or intellectual rights.

Generally, in this country, pollution is covered under a public liability policy. But the cover given is limited to bodily injury or property damage claims subject to the consequence being accidental. In recent years, as concern about the environment has increased it has been possible to get environmental impairment liability insurance. In addition to covering normal injury or property damage it also includes liability in the event of an impairment or diminution of or interference with any other right or amenity protected by law. However, such policies exclude war risks and nuclear risks, so an event such as at Chernobyl would not be protected. There are some exclusions which can be modified if appropriate underwriting information, premium and terms are available.

15 Lloyd's

Lloyd's is a unique British way of providing insurance. Here, anything can be insured. It is not a company and has no shareholders. It is a society of underwriters all of whom accept insurance risks for their personal profit or loss and are liable **to the full extent of their private wealth** to meet their insurance commitments.

The origin of Lloyd's

Its uniqueness lies in the way it functions, which, in turn, can be traced to its origins in the coffee houses of the 17th century. This was a time when coffee, having been introduced in the country just before the Civil War, was a very popular drink. The first coffee house was opened in London in 1652 and in 1688 Lloyd's Coffee House made its appearance in Tower Street, owned by one Edward Lloyd. Little is known about Lloyd or his coffee house but it does seem that from the beginning Lloyd encouraged a clientele of ships' captains, merchants, shipowners and others with an interest in overseas trade. Lloyd's coffee house gained an enviable reputation for trustworthy shipping news. This was one of the basic ingredients of successful underwriting and it soon became the recognised place for obtaining marine insurance.

Edward Lloyd himself did not underwrite – as far as we can tell. His coffee house was probably not the only place underwriting was done but it became the only place following the passage of the Bubble Act of 1720. This came in the wake of the South Sea Bubble scandal when thousands of investors were ruined. The Act granted charters to two companies, prohibiting marine insurance by any other corporation or business partnership. But the Act did not curb the underwriting activities of private individuals and it was this exclusion that really created Lloyd's.

Lloyd's today

Much has changed since those days. Lloyd's has had its own scandals and acts of Parliament to regulate its affairs but the basic principle of Lloyd's survives. A policy at Lloyd's is subscribed to by private individuals with unlimited liability. Today, nearly 29,000 members are grouped into approximately 370 syndicates varying in size from a few score to more than a thousand names. The affairs of each syndicate are managed by an underwriting agent who is responsible for appointing a professional underwriter for each main class of business.

Lloyd's, originally developed as a market for marine insurance, now derives well over half of its annual premium income of about £6,000 million from non-marine sources. Risk of every conceivable description, with the exception of life insurance for periods of more than ten years are accepted by Lloyd's underwriters from most countries either directly or by reinsurance. Lloyd's underwriters are estimated to cover one in seven private motorists in Great Britain and Lloyd's brokers are famous for insuring unusual risks. The insurance of a comedian's moustache, a wine taster's palate, or against the payment of a large prize in the event of someone catching the Loch Ness Monster, represent some of the events a Lloyd's broker may take on.

The essential business at Lloyd's is done in the underwriting room at Lloyd's—known simply as The Room where brokers and underwriters negotiate risks. The insurance broker is a key figure in the Lloyd's market. Lloyd's underwriters have no other contact with the insuring public and their premium income is entirely dependent on the initiative and enterprise of the Lloyd's broker in obtaining business throughout the world. There are some 260 or so accredited brokerage firms and their conduct is governed by high professional standards demanded by the Council of Lloyd's, established under the Lloyd's Act 1982 which is the government of Lloyd's and has overall responsibility for the control of the market.

16 What do they mean by . . .

Annuity

A sum of money paid at regular intervals to the policyholder.

Assurance

An arrangement by which something is promised or guaranteed.

Assured

A person who has a life assurance policy – also called the policyholder.

Assurer

The organisation which provides a person with assurance – also called the assurance company or life office.

Benefit

The money paid by the assurance company when a claim is made.

Bonus

The extra amount of money that is paid with the final benefit to a policyholder who has a with-profit policy.

Claim

The demand made by a policyholder, or his family, or next of kin for the agreed benefit to be paid by the assurance or insurance company.

Composite offices

These are offices which sell all types of policies: pensions life assurance and general assurance. So from one company you can get your car insurance, house insurance, life policy, pensions, and yacht insurance.

Deferred annuity

An annuity that is paid for by the policyholder over an agreed period of time before the annuity is due to start.

Endowment assurance

A life assurance policy that provides a sum of money either at the end of an agreed period of time, or on the death of the policyholder, depending on which of the two happens first.

Insurable interest

A person can only take out a policy on another person's life when he or she has a particular interest or financial involvement in the policy.

Insurance

An arrangement that offers a policyholder protection against something that may or may not occur.

Insurance broker

The person or organisation arranging policies that are on offer from the various companies. The Financial Services Act introduced two types of brokers. A company representative offers only the policies of a particular life assurance or insurance company. An independent financial advisor sets out to acquaint himself or herself with his or her client's financial position and offers the best advice on what kind of policy should be used.

Insurance company

An organisation that provides both insurance and life assurance policies.

Insured

A person who has an insurance policy – also called the policyholder.

Insurer

The organisation which provides a person with insurance – also called the insurance company.

Level premium

In life assurance the amount of the premium that a person pays does not change from year to year. It is agreed and fixed when the policy is first arranged, which means that the policyholder always knows how much his or her policy is going to cost.

Life expectancy

The length of time that a person is likely to live. This is calculated according to the person's age, health and occupation.

Life fund

The pool of money into which all life assurance policyholders' premiums are paid, and from which all benefits are eventually paid back.

Life office

An organisation that provides life assurance policies, also known as an assurance company.

Maturity date

An agreed date in the future when a policy comes to an end.

No further payments are required after that date, because the benefit is then paid by the assurance company.

Mortgage protection

A policy that is linked to a mortgage loan and which covers the policyholder for the amount of the mortgage that is owed to the building society.

Mutual office

This is owned by the policyholders and no outside shareholders participate in the profits.

No-claims bonus

This applies in general insurance, particularly motor insurance where, as a reward for not making a claim on the insurance company, the premium charged is reduced by a certain amount. This amount varies from company to company. There is also a protected no-claims bonus where even if a claim is made the bonus is not affected, provided that the number of claims do not exceed a certain figure. This again varies from company to company.

Non-commissioned office

Most life offices pay commission to third parties in some form or another. But some offices, such as Equitable Life, make a virtue of not paying commission to intermediaries such as brokers, accountants, etc.

Non-profit

The policyholder agrees to pay a certain sum of money to the life assurance company and it guarantees, in return, to pay a fixed amount either on death or at the end of a specified period.

Premium

The money paid for a policy. In the case of an assurance policy this is a fixed amount paid at regular intervals. In the case of an insurance policy, it is an amount that is paid each year and may change annually, according to the insurance that is required.

Proposal form

The form completed by a person applying for a policy.

Proposer

A person who has completed a proposal form. Once this is accepted by the assurance or insurance company and the first premium has been paid, the proposer becomes a policyholder.

Proprietary office

This is a life office which is owned by proprietors (who are generally shareholders) which can either be a private limited company or a plc, quoted on the stock exchange. Most of our big life companies are publicly quoted.

Risk

The chance that something unpleasant may happen. The greater the risk, the higher the premium needed to insure against it.

Self-administered

This is a method of investment used mainly for pension schemes in which the members and trustees of the scheme effectively control the investment policy of the scheme. Small self-administered pension schemes are restricted to less than 12 members – in effect small companies and partnerships. This allows the firm or partnership that has set up the scheme to borrow up to 50% of the value of the scheme for the purpose of the business.

Tax relief

Premiums paid on most life policies in force before 14 March 1984 attracted tax relief but policies since then do not enjoy this benefit.

Term or temporary assurance

This provides an agreed sum of money to be paid if the policyholder dies within an agreed period of time. Mortgage protection policies and family income benefit policies are both term insurances.

Unit-linked policies

A unit-linked policy links the policy to the underlying investments on stocks, gilts, property, etc, and the amount of money that such a policy pays will depend on the value of the underlying investment.

Utmost good faith

This phrase used in insurance means that a proposer or a policyholder is always honest and truthful in his or her dealings with an assurance or insurance company.

Whole life assurance

This provides for an agreed sum of money to be paid to the policyholder's family or next-of-kin when the policyholder dies, whenever that may be.

With-profit

A policy where the policyholder shares in the life company's investment returns. The share is worked out by the actuary of the company and can be distributed either in the form of a reversionary bonus, paid each year or a terminal bonus paid at the time of maturity. There is no knowing what sums of money a with-profits policy will yield.

Index

Other titles in this series:

Managing Your Finances	Helen Pridham
Planning Your Pension	Tony Reardon
Buying Your Home	Richard Newell
Running Your Own Business	David Williams
Your Home in Spain	Institute of Foreign Property Owners
Your Home in Portugal	Rosemary de Rougemont
Tax for the Self-Employed	David Williams
Investing in Shares	Hugh Pym & Nick Kochan
Planning School and College Fees	Danby Bloch & Amanda Pardoe
Leaving Your Money Wisely	Tony Foreman